Cat Women
of West Michigan
The Secret World of Cat Rescue

By Janet Vormittag

ISBN: 978-0-9986987-5-5

Published by JLV Enterprises, LLC
Cats and Dogs

Dedicated to all the women (and men) in
West Michigan who help cats.

Contents

Contents

Introduction

Back in the 1980s I volunteered at a local county animal shelter. I lasted one day. On that first and only day, an animal control officer brought in a pregnant cat. She was a beauty. A friendly tortoiseshell with black fur tinged with orange. She also had a bulging belly.

The woman who was training me explained that without a collar or any other sign of ownership, by law, the stray had to be held for three days. The calico had no signs of ownership other than she was super sweet.

"Will you put her in foster care to have her babies?" I asked.

She said, no. The shelter was already full of kittens. The woman hoped the cat wouldn't have her babies in the next three days—it was easier to euthanize a pregnant cat than it was to euthanize a mom with squirming babies.

I finished that day and never went back.

If you become involved in animal rescue, you soon learn of a fifth season. Besides spring, summer, fall and winter, there is kitten season when shelters and rescues are flooded with cute little fluff balls. Everyone who drops off a cardboard box full of lovely kittens hopes the shelter will find homes for the babies.

Who doesn't love kittens?

The problem is—what do you do with dozens and dozens of kittens when no one is coming to adopt?

The answer: you kill them.

I won't use the word euthanize. According to the *Encarta World English Dictionary*, the definition of euthanasia is *the act or practice of killing somebody who has an incurable illness or injury, or allowing or assisting that person to die.*

The majority of those kittens weren't sick or injured. There were just too many of them.

Don't blame the staff at the shelter for the killing. Blame the community. Blame yourself. The shelter staff is just doing the dirty work.

According to an article in *The Grand Rapids Press*, 9,762 cats and dogs were euthanized in Kent County in 1993. Kent County, the home of Grand Rapids, has two animal shelters: an open-admission, county-run animal shelter and a limited-admission humane society.

While I didn't go back to the county shelter to do hands-on work with homeless pets, I found another way to help. The shelter had doggie-shaped piggy banks in area businesses to collect people's spare change. I volunteered to exchange the full banks with empty banks. I'd count the change, roll it and turn it into the shelter.

In 2006, I combined my passions for helping animals and writing and founded *Cats and Dogs, a Magazine Devoted to Companion Animals*. The free publication, made possible thanks to advertisers, featured animals available for adoption at area shelters and rescues. The content also included fun and educational articles about cats, dogs and other animals.

Every year I printed statistics from area shelters. How many animals were taken in, how many were returned to their owners, how many were adopted, how many were transferred to other shelters or rescues, and how many were (there's that word again) euthanized.

In 2006, the number of cats and dogs euthanized in Kent County was 7,711: 5,547 were cats and 2,164 were dogs. These numbers don't include owner requested euthanasia.

Over the years, adoptions, return-to-owners and transfers have steadily increased while animal intake and euthanasia have decreased.

In 2020, the number of cats and dogs euthanized in Kent County was 253: 119 were cats and 134 were dogs.

One of the reasons for the improved numbers is West Michigan has low-cost spay/neuter clinics. In addition, there are dozens of rescue groups. Besides finding homes for pets, members of the groups help educate the public about the importance of adoption, spay/neuter and microchipping.

There are also organizations devoted to trap-neuter-return (TNR) of feral cats. In TNR, cats are live-trapped, spayed/neutered and returned to where they were caught. They live out their lives, but they don't reproduce.

While publishing *Cats and Dogs Magazine*, I've met countless women, and a few men, who work tirelessly to improve the lives of animals in West Michigan and beyond.

In this book, you'll meet a few of the women who have dedicated themselves to helping cats and kittens. There are dozens of women in West Michigan who help cats. Unfortunately, all their stories wouldn't fit into one book. I've limited this book to the women I've met through my work with the magazine.

Believe me, there are numerous women who are worthy of being included in this book. There are also dozens of women who are dedicated to helping both cats and dogs, and several women who work only with dogs. Plus, there are those who help wildlife and farm animals, and others who help other critters such as ferrets, rabbits, guinea pigs and the various other animals kept as pets.

I'm thankful for everyone who helps make the lives of animals better.

Chapter 1

Women Who Start Cat Rescues

Every cat rescue in West Michigan is run by a woman. Why? I don't know. A few of them are married with supportive husbands, but the wives are the driving force. Some have children, some don't. Most, but not all, are employed. Some are retired.

It takes an exceptional woman to start and manage a cat rescue. She is most likely strong-minded, independent, tough, tenacious, intelligent and energetic. She has grit. She knows how to run a business and manage people. She has the social skills necessary to motivate volunteers, to develop relationships with veterinarians, and to convince the community to adopt, spay/neuter and donate. She knows how to raise funds and budget money.

Plus, she needs to be a walking encyclopedia regarding kittens and cats. How to keep them healthy. How to recognize diseases, parasites and trauma. How to render basic first aid, administer fluids, socialize feral kittens and so much more.

She must be tough enough to make life and death decisions. How much money is spent trying to save the life of one cat? Especially, when money is tight and that same money could be used to spay/neuter several cats. Are pregnant cats spayed, knowing the unborn kittens will be sacrificed during the procedure? Can she say no to a cat in need when every cage and every foster is full? Especially a cat scheduled to be euthanized?

In this chapter, you'll meet women who run or have started cat rescues. Some of those rescues are going strong after years of operation, but a few have closed. Thankfully, several new cat rescues have emerged to carry on the work.

Cat rescue seems to be never ending.

Carol Manos with her boy Gus.

Is there Life after Cats?

Carol Manos described herself as broke, fat, addicted to food, mentally ill and suicidal.

"I'm unrecognizable as the person I once was," she said.

Carol was once a professional woman in retail management, but then she got involved in rescue.

I first met Carol when I interviewed her in 2007 for an article about Carol's Ferals, an organization she had founded the year before. Her mission was to end cat overpopulation in West Michigan.

Twelve years later, I was interviewing her again. She welcomed me into her condo on the northeast side of Grand Rapids where we chatted and sipped tea. Later she served a lunch of vegan keto chili.

"I've always loved cats, always cared about animal welfare," she said. She protested the seal hunts in Canada and stood up for the underdog nerds in school. "I have a big mouth and gave it to the voiceless."

Fifteen years after starting the cat rescue that bore her name, Carol struggled with separating herself from the organization. She was in search of the woman she remembered from long ago. Therapy was helping her analyze her life. Looking back, Carol could see the key events that led her to cat rescue.

As an only child, Carol said she was adored, spoiled and loved by her parents. Carol's mother had 11 miscarriages, which made the miracle of her birth even more precious. When Carol's dad, Paris Manos, died Dec. 26, 2005, Carol lost her grounding. Her mother had passed two and a half years earlier, so with her dad's passing Carol had no one to tell her how special she was. And she craved those words.

"I was looking for something that gave me that good feeling, but the strokes turned to punches and I got beat up," she said with tears in her eyes.

She recalled how she got started in cat rescue. When Hurricane Katrina hit, Carol and her friend Gabby drove their RV to the Gulf Coast to help animals. Carol recalls seeing a pickup truck that had "animal rescue" painted on its back window and thinking of the rescuers as gods.

Back in Grand Rapids, she heard about cats eating out of a Dumpster at a Burger King in Cutlerville. She bought a live trap for $60 and started trapping. She wrote a blog, *Fast Food Feral Felines,* and used her creative voice to advocate for outside cats.

Then she heard about a trailer park in Cedar Springs that was overrun with cats. She attacked the project with gusto, going door-to-door in the park offering spay/neuter services and trapping outside cats. Some of the cats tested positive for feline leukemia. Dr. Jen, who ran Big Sid's, a rescue that specialized in cats with feline leukemia and FIV, took the cats who tested positive.

"She became my savior," Carol recalled.

Altogether, close to 100 cats from the trailer park were spayed or neutered and tested for the disease.

Carol also volunteered for C-SNIP, a low-cost spay/ neuter clinic in West Michigan. She learned pregnant cats were spayed, which aborted the unborn kittens. "It upset me," she recalled. But then she learned cats were prolific breeders, and that thousands of cats and kittens were euthanized at area shelters because there weren't enough homes for all of them.

"One intact female and her mates have the breeding potential to create 11,000 cats over five years," Carol said. She said kittens born outside had a low survival rate. They froze to death, were killed by predators, starved, succumbed to disease or fell victim to humans who poisoned, shot, and trapped to kill.

So, she founded Carol's Ferals and began a crusade to end the overpopulation of cats. Her specialty was trap-neuter-return (TNR). Cats were live-trapped, taken for spay/neuter surgery and then returned to where they were caught. The cats were also ear-tipped, a universal sign that an outside cat has been spayed/neutered.

In 2008, Carol's Ferals became a 501(c)(3) nonprofit organization.

Carol believed in the cause to the point of spending $35,000 of her own money. For 12½ years she devoted her life to cats, never getting paid. She put in 60-80 hours per week.

"It snowballed," she said.

She estimated Carol's Ferals spayed or neutered close to 11,800 cats. Of those, 1,900 were adopted into new homes.

"I led a life of great purpose for years," she said.

Carol credits several groups for making it all possible. In the beginning, Vicky's Pet Connection helped pay for surgeries. Veterinarian Bruce Langlois gave her a discounted rate for spaying/neutering feral cats. He didn't limit the number of cats she could bring and extended her credit when needed. He also rented her a facility where she could have an office, house cats available for adoption, store equipment, do intake for trapped cats, and have space for cats to recuperate before being returned outside.

Just like the events that led her into cat rescue, Carol could see the events that caused her to step back from rescue.

Dr. Langlois was accused of malpractice and eventually lost his license to practice veterinary medicine. With him went her access to affordable, convenient veterinary care. Dr. Langlois's accusers were "rescue people," who Carol once held in high esteem, which caused a fracture in the rescue community.

Another event that led to Carol's decision to leave rescue was a call from someone about a cat they found frozen to death in a live trap at Sandy Pines, a resort community south of Grand Rapids. Carol tried to find justice for the cat, but she said people were more concerned about their property values than the cat. No one was held accountable for setting the trap in killer-cold temperatures and not checking it to see if an animal had been caught.

Then there were the endless telephone calls, emails and Facebook requests for help. "I don't want to give any more of my heart to the pain," she said.

Even when she was at her breaking point, Carol still stayed three more years. Fists clenched, wanting to punch someone, she self-medicated with food. She estimated she gained and lost close to 400 pounds during her years in cat rescue.

But she still loves cats. She lives with the unadoptable misfit cats who somehow made their way to Carol's Ferals. One cat was hit by a car and shot with a pellet gun, which resulted in a leg amputation and incontinence. She has a diabetic cat who needs injections twice a day. Another has hyperthyroid, causing him to be hungry all the time and in need of meds every 12 hours.

When we talked, Carol was slowly stepping back from Carol's Ferals and had started turning over the day-to-day operations to a trusted friend. She wanted to still be involved in fundraising and operational decisions.

Carol worried about what her life would be without being consumed with cat rescue.

"There's more to me than cats, but most of my friends

are from cat rescue. I hope they still like me on the other side. When I come through this."

Part of Carol's new life is buying and selling antiques and collectibles, something she used to do with her parents. Recently she stopped at a second-hand shop on Plainfield Avenue and spotted an old Avon perfume decanter. It stopped her in her tracks.

In Carol's basement, there is a memory shelf dedicated to her parents. One of the treasured items is an Avon elephant cologne bottle that is missing its head. Carol explained that her father and she used to play a game of find-the-head. One of them would hide the elephant's head in a place where the other person would eventually stumble upon it. For example, one summer Carol put the head in the pocket of her Father's winter coat. He didn't find it until the weather turned cold. They played the hide-and-seek game for three decades until his death. "I buried the head with my father," Carol said.

She never came across another Avon elephant—until she stopped at the store on Plainfield. The day after Christmas and the 14th anniversary of her Father's death.

When she saw the cologne bottle, she knew it was more than a coincidence.

"I haven't had a sign from my parents, but I haven't had my eyes open," she said. Instead of grieving her parents' death she threw herself into cat rescue. Now that she was slowing down she was able to connect with them.

"They're still with me. I'm going to be okay."

Update: In 2021, Carol realized she needed to take care of herself and decided to close Carol's Ferals. In 15 years, Carol's Ferals sterilized more than 12,000 cats, found homes for close to 2,000 friendly cats and found safe outdoor environments for more than 300 cats who couldn't be returned to where they were caught.

Jen Kuyt with Jitter Bug.

Therapy Cats

When Jen Kuyt's husband lay claim to the pole barn at their new home in Wayland, Jen announced she wanted the two-stall garage that was adjacent to the building.

"He asked me what I was going to do with it, and I joked that I was going to fill it with cats," she said.

At first Jen thought she might use the space to provide a home for unadoptable cats or perhaps a feral cat colony. But then she took her special-needs son to H.U.G.S. Ranch in Byron Center for a session of therapeutic horseback riding. While there, she noticed another child playing with barn cats. That's when the idea came to her—*why not use cats for therapy?*

"It snowballed from there—I knew the direction I wanted to go," Jen said. She decided to rescue pregnant/ nursing cats and orphaned kittens and raise the babies to be therapy or emotional support pets.

Jen applied for a 501(c)(3) nonprofit status and researched how to lay out the 600-square-foot garage to optimize the space. She applied for a license from the Michigan Department of Agriculture, which oversees animal rescues.

The Country Cat Lady opened in May 2019. "We're not a shelter. We're a sanctuary," Jen said. Kittens who don't have the personality for therapy or emotional support work are available for adoption as are mom cats.

Jen has developed a *Last Litter Program*. When she has the space, she takes in pregnant cats from people who don't want kittens. After the cats raise their babies, the moms are spayed and returned to their owners.

"Kittens are so much healthier when their mom raises them," Jen explained, but she does have foster homes where orphaned kittens are bottle-fed and hand raised.

The renovated garage has a lobby, three rooms for free-roaming cats and a room for a nursing mom. Jen also has a nursery in her home.

Jen has about 40 volunteers who help with daily chores, application approvals, fostering and socializing kittens. As a mother of a special-needs son, Jen knows the importance of giving everyone an opportunity to volunteer. Her volunteers have different levels of capabilities and she doesn't expect perfection.

Cats help kids work on their social skills. "It helps them understand the untold social story so many special-needs kids struggle with," she explained. For example, if a child is too loud or rambunctious a cat will run away. If they want to play with the cat, they learn to be quiet and sit still.

Kittens with "elite" personalities are available for adoption as emotional support pets and are excellent companions for people who deal with depression or anxiety.

Since the Country Cat Lady opened, Jen has adopted out close to 380 cats as of July 2022. She has placed emotional support cats as far away as Chicago. She's had requests for cats from Europe, New York City and Georgia, but doesn't want her cats to travel that far.

Currently Jen has 50 cats in her care and more than 40 in foster homes.

Jen takes cats and kittens to Green Acres, an assisted living facility in Wayland. She sets up a large screened playpen where the kittens can run loose. Some residents just like to watch their playful antics. When the kittens calm down, they're allowed out to interact with people.

"When I leave, I have to take sleeping kittens out of people's hands," Jen said.

During the Covid-19 shutdown, Jen walked outside the windows of Green Acres with one of her therapy cats. Some residents teared-up just seeing her and the cat.

Jen also runs a Reading with Cats program at the local library.

While Jen loves cats, her true passion is for people. "People drive my vision, not animals, but the cats get 100 percent of what they need," she said.

Jen has partnered with Allegan County's Hillsdale Transition Center, which helps young adults with a variety of disabilities. The Center offers programs that help strengthen their abilities to navigate in their communities and fully participate in family activities. A focus is placed on vocational skills.

Small groups of the young adults come to the Country Cat Lady's facility and help with small chores and interact with the cats.

Jen's next goal is to create a Community Center in Wayland. Her plan is to connect the community through cats. "We'll use cats to create fellowship," she explained.

Jen is looking for a building close to downtown that can be used for multiple activities. It will have an adoption room for cats and space for after-school programs for students. Library staff will be able to hold programs in the Center since the library is in a small historical building with limited space. The Hillsdale Transition Center can bring young adults to practice job skills. "They need repetitive practice to be employable and independent," she explained.

An anonymous supporter has agreed to purchase a building for the Center. Besides searching for the perfection location, Jen is looking for sponsors to help with operational expenses.

Jen already has a mascot for the Center. Jitter Bug, a four-week-old black and white kitten, had been found alone in someone's yard. The young cat has cerebellar hypoplasia (CH), a development condition sometimes called wobbly cat syndrome, where the part of the brain that controls fine motor skills, balance and coordination fails to develop. Symptoms can include jerky walking, swaying, tremors and falling down. There is no treatment, and cats with CH adapt to their disability.

Jen explained that having a cat with a disability as the Center's mascot will be a good teaching tool. "Just because we're different doesn't mean we're loved any less," she said.

For more information visit www.countrycatlady.org.

Dr. Amy Pietras with a foster kitten who
needed extra medical attention.

The World Needs Fewer Animals

In early 2005, Amy Pietras started Jandy's Home, a nonprofit dedicated to cats. Her original intent was humane education—to help teachers integrate humane treatment of animals into whichever subject they taught.

"Then Katrina happened, and I changed gears entirely," Amy said. Katrina, a category five hurricane, made landfall on the Gulf Coast in August 2005.

Mark Steinway, a man involved in animal rescue who Amy followed online, wrote about the work being done to help displaced cats and dogs in New Orleans. She was so moved by his writings that she quit her job as a CPA, packed up her car and drove by herself to Louisiana to lend a hand. For ten days she helped rescue and care for abandoned pets.

Cats displaced by the hurricane were soon having kittens. "Spay/neuter was like a foreign language down there," Amy said. She made several trips to New Orleans and began bringing back cats and kittens. She estimated she transported close to 300 kittens to Grand Rapids. Through Jandy's Home, she found homes for them, but not before they were thoroughly vetted. All the cats and kittens were tested for feline leukemia and FIV, received full sets of vaccines, treated for parasites, spayed/neutered and microchipped.

Amy also got involved in TNR in West Michigan. Working in rescue gave her an insight. "The world doesn't need more animal groups. It needs fewer animals."

Amy decided to return to school to become a veterinarian. She especially wanted to learn shelter medicine and how to do spay/neuter surgeries. She applied to the College of Veterinary Medicine at Michigan State University and was accepted. The next four years were "the most hideous time in my life." The daily commute from her home in Alto to East Lansing was close to an hour one way—she'd be gone eight to ten hours every day. At the time, she had more than two dozen of her own animals who needed care and attention. Plus, there was studying to do.

"There was no time for anything pleasant," she said.

But the sacrifices were worthwhile. Amy received her diploma in 2017, and soon after she started the Quick Fix Veterinary Clinic. The non-profit clinic offers low-cost services, including spay/neuter surgery. It serves animal welfare organizations, rescues, cat colony caretakers and anyone who can't afford a full-service veterinary clinic or is unable to get a timely appointment with a regular veterinarian.

Dr. Amy spayed/neutered more than 2,000 cats for Muskegon's Heaven Can Wait in 2021.

Dr. Amy credits studying economics as part of the reason she can keep her prices low. "All the stuff I learned—business, taxes, accounting—play a major role in where I am today," she said. She buys smart, buys in bulk, and doesn't pay for office space. Instead she works where she lives to keep the overhead low.

"It's the ultimate work at home," she said. Her bedroom was transformed into a surgical room and the great room into a holding and recovery area.

"I kicked myself out of my own bedroom," she joked. She now bunks in the clinic's office.

On the clinic's Facebook page, Dr. Amy shares her work days. One day in June she and her crew spayed/ neutered 70 cats for Heaven Can Wait and did one dental. A photo shows her great room with cat carriers wall-to-wall, some double stacked.

Another day, Dr. Amy and her helpers performed 75 spay/neuter surgeries, three wellness visits including vaccines, a dental, and treated an injured barn cat and a litter of kittens who needed flea treatment and deworming. The last person left at 8 p.m., and then she set up cages for 14 sick surrendered cats who would be coming the following week. The day also included treating a neighbor's outside cat who was vomiting. The post concluded that she didn't always return phone calls or answer emails in a timely fashion due to the long, busy days.

Dr. Amy isn't driven by money; instead, she does what she believes is right for every animal. "I don't euthanize because someone can't afford to pay. No animal comes in here with a condition that we can treat and leaves with it untreated. I make vaccines part of spay/neuter and if people try to opt out, they get a lecture."

The consent form pet owners sign states that she can treat any condition. Cats with ear mites, worms or any other parasites get treated. She's a big believer in dentals for pets.

Dr. Amy also works weekends and holidays to accommodate pet owners who can't get paid time off from work. She can work non-traditional hours because she's single and doesn't have children. Plus, she loves what she does.

It took Dr. Amy a long time to figure out what makes her happy. She realized she couldn't do only one thing. She loves variety—spay/neuter surgeries two or three days a week and wellness clinics the other days. She enjoys traveling and has gone to Greece to help with spay/neuter clinics, and she regularly goes to Virginia to help in a surgical unit. She also travels around Michigan to do spay/neuter clinics.

Dr. Amy has always been a cat woman. "My mom would say from birth," she joked. It started with the family cat Nosey, a big white and gray tiger who had his nose in everything. She has pictures of herself as a child sleeping with Nosey.

Occasionally, Dr. Amy works with dogs, but she

focuses on cats because the biggest problem in Michigan is cat over population. "Michigan doesn't have a dog population problem. We have an unwanted dog population problem," she said, explaining that dogs in shelters are usually not the type of pet people want. The reasons vary—the dogs are older, untrained, large breeds or pit bull mixes.

When asked about the burnout rate in rescue, Amy acknowledged the high suicide rate among veterinarians. But doing what she wants, when she wants is mentally beneficial. "It doesn't seem like work when you set your own schedule, but I keep my CPA license up to date. It's nice for a backup."

For information visit http://www.quickfixvet.com or follow Quick Fix Veterinary Clinic on Facebook.

Michelle and Tom Hocking

We're in this Together

From my vantage point, not many men are involved in cat rescue. They are a rare breed, kind of like male calico cats—only .1 percent of calico cats are male. One guy involved in cat rescue is Tom Hocking. When asked why he devotes his spare time to cats, Tom said it was because his wife's heart is in cat rescue. The fact that he loves cats is secondary to helping Michelle.

"We're in this together," Michelle said.

I visited with the Hockings at their Kitty Kabin, a 1,300 square foot building built near their home. We sat in the just-completed catio, where cats lounged on catwalks, in the rafters and on furniture designed for felines.

In November 2013, Tom and Michelle started Cannonsville Critters, a non-profit, no-kill cat rescue in Montcalm County named after the road they lived on. The couple rescue abandoned, abused and neglected cats and kittens. Their goal is to reduce the euthanasia rate at the county shelter.

"We had no idea what we were getting into," Michelle said. At one time they had 50 cats in the basement of their home. When there wasn't enough room in the house, they started placing cats in their garage. Then they built the Kitty Kabin.

The Kitty Kabin has rooms for free-roaming cats, a quarantine room, storage space, laundry and a bathroom. It also has a room where a veterinarian can do checkups on the residents. What was supposed to be an office for Michelle became another cat room. Her office is now in a large closet with no windows, but she doesn't mind.

Pet incubators are their newest acquisitions. The incubators have temperature and humidity controls, which are life-saving for orphaned kittens who don't have a mother to cuddle with for warmth. At the time of our interview, which was during kitten season, Cannonsville Critters had 172 kittens in their program, of which 100 were in foster homes.

Before starting the rescue, Michelle volunteered for Lake Haven Rescue, a no-kill rescue in neighboring Newaygo County. Before that she volunteered for the Montcalm County Animal Shelter. She recalled the day she transported kittens from the county shelter to Lake Haven and met the rescue's founder and director Cheryl McCloud.

"She asked me if I wanted to foster a Saint Bernard," Michelle said with a laugh. "A Saint Bernard!" The request stunned her, but she said yes, and that was the start of a three-year stint of volunteering for Lake Haven.

"I learned a lot from Cheryl," Michelle said.

Michelle never intended to start a rescue, but the situation for cats in her home county wasn't good. "We needed more for the kitties," she said. "I didn't know what I was doing, but I did it anyways." The Montcalm County Animal Shelter primarily dealt with dogs and had only a small room for cats, and not many cats were being adopted.

I was thrilled when I heard someone was starting a cat rescue in Montcalm County. Years ago, I participated in demonstrations at the county's administrative building protesting the contract the county had with a USDA Class B Animal Dealer. The contract allowed the dealer to take shelter pets, which he sold to research facilities and universities that used animals in experiments and teaching labs. Eventually, the county didn't renew the contract.

Four of my cats are from Montcalm—fosters cats who didn't get adopted. So, yes, I was thrilled to hear a rescue dedicated to cats was starting in that county. A lot of other people were also happy and several stepped up with advice and help.

Michelle said she had several mentors; Mary Ellen Snyder from Safe Haven Humane Society in Ionia County, Diane Valk from Heaven Can Wait in Muskegon and Jeanine Buckner from Reuben's Room Cat Rescue in Grand Rapids.

The couple also had built-in help—they had five children, four sons and a daughter, who all loved cats.

Three sons are now married and out on their own, and their daughter is moving Out West. Only one son remains at home.

Michelle is surprised by the support Cannonsville Critters receives from the community. "People want to help," she said, almost in disbelief. People donate money, supplies and items for resale. In addition, they foster and adopt. The group has 15 volunteers who help in any way they can.

Cannonsville Critters has cats and kittens available for adoption in Pet Supplies Plus stores in the Grand Rapids area. Michelle and Tom also hold monthly adoption events at local stores such as Tractor Supply Co. in Greenville. At a recent event Tom said he left for a bit and when he returned there was a line of people. He wondered, *why the line*? Turned out people were in line to adopt kittens.

"We adopted out 45 kittens that day," Michelle said. It set a record for the number of adoptions in one day. Which is good, because one day during kitten season a woman brought them a cardboard box filled with three mom cats and more than a dozen kittens. Every day they get calls for cats and kittens in need of help.

Cannonsville Critters has adopted out more than 3,200 cats in the nine years since they started. All the cats are fully vetted—they're tested for diseases, spayed/neutered, up to date on vaccines, treated for parasites, and receive dentals, if needed.

As with every rescue, fundraising is never-ending. "We fundraise all the time," Michelle said. The group holds yard sales twice a year. Michelle reminisced about the early days of doing outside sales. She laughed at the memory of trying to dry stuff after a sudden downpour. They've come a long way—they now have tents.

Besides yard sales, funding comes from adoption fees, grants, Facebook fundraisers and monthly donations from supporters.

"We've never been not able to pay our bills," Michelle said.

Businesses within the county are also supportive. The owners of Kaleidoscope of Times, an antique mall in Greenville, gave the group a booth where they can sell donated items. "They do a huge amount for us," Michelle said, adding that they are allowed to park trailers at the mall so people can drop off yard-sale donations and returnable cans and bottles.

Another supporter is the local Family, Farm & Home store, which donates food, making it possible for the group to feed the colonies of cats they have trapped, neutered, and returned. TNR is something they would like to do more of in the future.

Tom said the best thing about being in rescue is hearing from people who have adopted. A teenage girl, whose parents let her and her brother each adopt a kitten during the Covid-19 pandemic, wrote saying how much she loved the cats and how much she appreciated Cannonsville Critters.

"That's the best part for me too," Michelle said.

When asked about the not-so-good side of rescue,

Tom recalled an orange tabby named Mr. Orange who they hoped would not get adopted. Mr. Orange loved to give hugs—he would wrap his front legs around your neck and hug. One day, a woman whose cat had died came to adopt. Mr. Orange hugged her and through tears she said, "He's the one." Both Tom and Michelle didn't want to let him go, but they knew the woman would give him a wonderful home. The memory of Mr. Orange made them emotional.

Another cat who stole their hearts was Kai, a young cat someone had found outside and was diagnosed with water on the brain. Kai lost his ability to walk and had to wear diapers. "He became my buddy. I took him everywhere," Michelle said. After two years of being a pampered pet, Kai had a seizure and didn't recover.

The lowest side of rescue for the Hockings is when people are cruel to cats. They've helped at homes of hoarders where cats were found dead or suffering.

Michelle also feels bad when people get upset with her—usually because she has to tell them she can't help because the rescue is full.

"We have to turn a lot of people down," she said.

"We make a lot of people mad," Tom added.

Michelle said that's when she needs Tom the most. He's calm and able to take everything in stride.

"He keeps me going," she said.

For information visit www.cannonsvillecritters.org. You can also follow them on Facebook.

Dr. Jen Gillum with Hudson, a patient at
Feline Wellness Center.

Every Cat Gets a Name

For twenty years Crash's Landing has been a cornerstone of the cat rescue community in Grand Rapids. Crash's was founded in 2002 by Jen Gillum, DVM.

Dr. Jen was converted to a cat person when she became a veterinarian. "It's in my blood now. It's my passion," she told me.

Rescuing cats started shortly after she graduated in 1995 from the College of Veterinary Medicine at Purdue University. She had no place to take strays so she took them home. With a husband, two young sons and family pets, their home eventually became crowded. Dr. Jen moved the strays to an old barber shop she purchased on the west side of Grand Rapids. Before the move, she decided to start a nonprofit for cats.

Crash's Landing was named after an eight-week-old black kitten who had been hit by a car in 1999. A good Samaritan brought him to Dr. Jen at Clyde Park Veterinary Clinic. The two-pound kitten had three fractured legs, a shattered foot and a broken tail that had to be amputated. The lucky kitty survived and Dr. Jen named him Crash—he had crash landed and had no place to go. Crash became the shelter's mascot and part of the organization's logo.

Over the years, Dr. Jen has fine-tuned the mission of Crash's Landing to primarily helping adult street cats who are sick or injured.

"The ones who need the most care," she said. "I'm in a unique position. I can do the work myself."

In 2004, Dr. Jen founded a second rescue, Big Sid's Sanctuary, which caters to cats who test positive for the FIV or FeLV viruses.

FIV (feline immunodeficiency virus) is comparable to HIV in humans. It's a slow virus that affects a cat's immune system over a period of years. Infected cats can often live long, healthy and relatively normal lives. FeLV (feline leukemia) can cause anemia, cancer and other illnesses, but infected cats can live many healthy years.

Big Sid's was named after a stray tomcat who tested positive for both viruses. Big Sid only lived seven weeks after his arrival, but he inspired Dr. Jen to do more for cats diagnosed with the viruses. A positive test usually resulted in euthanasia. Big Sid's was the first rescue in West Michigan devoted to cats with FIV and FeLV. Today other rescues also have rooms devoted to cats who carry the viruses.

Although a few of the Big Sid's cats are permanent residents, all of the Crash cats are available for adoption.

In May 2021, Crash's Landing and Big Sid's moved to a larger facility in Tallmadge Township, a few miles west of Grand Rapids. It has space for 25 Crash cats and 50 Sid's kids. It's the fourth move for Crash's Landing.

With the cats moved out of the old shelter, Dr. Jen made a huge decision on what to do with the vacant building. "It was an opportunity I couldn't pass up," she said. After working at Clyde Park Veterinary Clinic for almost 25 years, she decided to open her own practice in Crash's former home on Diamond Avenue. After months of renovations, Feline Wellness Center opened in January 2022. The cats-only center has a room set aside for cats from Crash and Big Sid's who need medical attention.

At the time of my visit, Dr. Jen was treating a cat with a dislocated jaw, a flea allergy, worms and who was lactating. Someone had seen the cat being chased by a fox. They intervened and brought the rescued cat to Dr. Jen, but they couldn't find the kittens. Dr. Jen named her Liza Skinelli, as she was missing the majority of the fur from the back of her head and shoulders. She has since been placed into a home with a volunteer.

Not all the cats brought in can be saved, but they die loved and with dignity. "I'll never euthanize a cat without giving them a name. They deserve that. They don't die alone. They don't die in pain," Dr. Jen said. In fact, Dr. Jen takes it upon herself to name every cat who comes into Crash's Landing and Big Sid's. She estimates she has named close to 4,300 cats. "I think about every name. It has to have meaning, and I never repeat names."

In the 20 years that Dr. Jen has been rescuing cats, she said one of the changes she has noticed has been the development of a network of rescues and community members dedicated to helping cats.

She mentioned Sandi DeHann, whom she nicknamed Southside Sandi. "She's a super hero," Dr. Jen said. Sandi (you'll meet her in a later chapter) does TNR and feeds several colonies of cats on the south side of Grand Rapids. When Sandi finds a cat with severe medical needs, she takes it to Dr. Jen.

It truly takes a village to help all the cats in need. Over the years, Dr. Jen has established a village of volunteers and supporters.

"We have amazing followers," she said. "It's amazing the support we get."

Close to 200 people volunteer at Crash's Landing and Big Sid's. While it's great for the cats, it can also be life changing for those who step up to help. Dr. Jen told the story of a love connection—one woman met her future husband at Crash's. In addition, nine women were influenced in their choices of careers: six studied to become veterinarian technicians and three to become veterinarians.

Crash's Landing and Big Sid's are primarily funded through private donations, including by individuals who sponsor a cat with monthly contributions. If there is a need for supplies, it's posted on social media and supporters order, and have sent, whatever the need is.

After years of operation, Crash's Landing and Big Sid's

run on schedules and devotion. With a reliable support staff, Dr. Jen doesn't have to give time to the rescues' daily operations. Which is good since she's putting in 12 or more hours per day at the Feline Wellness Center. Most of her work for the rescues is now behind-the-scenes. Besides the medical work, she writes thank-you notes to donors, writes the bios of the cats and does data entry.

Wednesdays and evenings, if needed, are set aside for Crash cats. "For me, it's the most gratifying. They come in at death's door. I get them healthy so they can thrive and be adopted," she said.

For more information visit www.crashslanding.org or follow Crash's Landing on Facebook.

Jeanine Buckner with Farmer Todd and Mazey.

Cats as a Lifestyle

Jeanine Buckner's first memory is being about five years old. A friendly stray cat she and her mom had been feeding had kittens in a garage lean-to. "Instead of one cat we had six," she recalled. She remembers the excitement of watching a mom-cat nursing her babies. That exhilaration turned to grief when a neighbor's dog killed the entire family.

"That memory haunts me. It's always with me," Jeanine said.

That childhood trauma was the seed of Jeanine's obsession with cats. Jeanine's dad was not an animal person so there were no pets in the family home, but she made up for the lack of childhood animal companions when she got her first apartment.

"If the humane society knew how many cats I had, I would have gone to jail," she said. Having a house full of cats became her normal. "I can't think of anything better than having a cat on your lap—or two or three."

To make a living, Jeanine worked in a dental office, but she jumped at the opportunity to volunteer at her veterinarian's office, Schmidt's Animal Hospital in Walker. Volunteering led to a paid position.

"I loved it. Loved it. Loved it," she said.

She credits a client, Michael O'Connor, with her decision to start a rescue. She remembers Michael telling her, "If you don't follow your dream, you'll always regret it and wish that you had."

She started down the path toward that dream by doing paperwork to become a 501(c)(3) non-profit. When the legal form asked for the name of the organization, Jeanine didn't have one. She thought of several cats the rescue could be named after and settled on one of Michael's cats, Reuben, who had lost an eye after being shot by a neighborhood kid with a BB gun.

Reuben's Room Rescue became official in 2003.

Jeanine said every rescue has its own mission. Hers is to take in domesticated cats when their people die or if they move where they aren't allowed to have cats. Reuben's Room doesn't take in strays, nor does it take in kittens under six months.

In 2005, Jeanine bought a house in Walker and received a special-use permit to use part of it as a rescue. The garage was converted into a comfortable place for cats waiting for their forever homes. There are windows to look out, cubbyholes to sleep in, toys to swat around and plenty of comfy beds. Cats are kept in large cages until they are comfortable in their new surroundings. Then the cage doors are left open and the cats can decide when they want to join the rest of the gang in the free-roam room.

The house's breezeway is used for laundry and for storage of litter, food and clean bedding.

"Every dollar donated goes to food, litter or vet bills," Jeanine said. Since the rescue is at her home, Jeanine pays the utilities. Everyone who helps with the cats, including herself, is a volunteer.

In 2006, when I decided to start a magazine about pets, my friend Bobbie Taylor told me I had to meet a friend of hers. Bobbie invited me to a cat show where this friend had an information table. That friend was Jeanine and the rescue was Reuben's Room Cat Rescue.

Jeanine told me about her rescue. I told her about my idea for a local pet magazine. She loved the idea and has been a supporter and friend ever since.

Reuben's Room is no-kill. Cats stay until they find a home. Jeanine's motto is, *Once a Reuben's Room cat, always a Reuben's Room cat*. Which means she always takes a cat back—no questions asked.

But most adoptions are long-term because Jeanine works hard to match each cat with the right family. She does home visits and each adoption is a trial-run for two weeks to make sure it's a good fit. Only then are the final adoption papers signed.

Reuben's Room adopts out about 50 cats a year.

While the converted garage houses rescue cats available for adoption, the rest of the house houses Jeanine's cat. A few of Jeanine's four-legged friends are *sanctuary* cats—unadoptable cats, either from old age, behavioral issues or medical problems who will live out their lives with Jeanine.

"No one is going to adopt them. People want kittens or younger cats," Jeanine explained. Her living room is a jungle of cat trees. They stretch from floor to ceiling and are placed in front of the windows for the best viewing. Cats can climb, hide, nap or bird watch.

Jeanine eventually got a job as a veterinarian assistant at the Kentwood Cat Clinic, a job she loved because it was all cats—no dogs. She admits she has a bigger heart for purring friends rather than barking ones.

While working at the cat clinic, Jeanine met clients who needed help medicating cats at home. So, she started *The Cats Meow*, which specializes in in-home cat care. She can help give pills, insulin injections or help with other minor medical situations. Jeanine also takes care of cats when their owners are on vacation.

When Jeanine built up a large enough clientele for her cat-care business, she left the Kentwood Cat Clinic and started supporting herself through *The Cats Meow*.

When everyone else looks forward to holidays as a break from work, Jeanine gears up—holidays are her busiest time. She squeezes in Thanksgiving dinners, opening Christmas gifts, and July 4th backyard barbecues between client visits. Jeanine's friends and family, including a daughter, son-in-law, and two grandchildren, have learned to accept her busy holiday schedule.

Cat rescue and in-home cat care were a winning

combination. People who adopted cats often become clients, and clients often adopted. Jeanine's trademark working attire is always a medical smock made from material sporting a cat design. She's seldom seen in anything else because her work is her lifestyle. She wouldn't have it any other way.

Jeanine isn't offended being called a Crazy Cat Lady. "I love it. It's the truth."

She finds satisfaction in saving cats from euthanasia. It used to be a death sentence when an older cat was no longer wanted—older cats are the first to be euthanized when an animal shelter runs out of space.

"The gratification of having a rescue comes from helping animals have a quality life and meeting like-minded people who become friends for life," she said.

Jeanine loves what she is doing and has never regretted taking Michael's advice of following her dream and starting a rescue.

"When I'm sitting in a rocker in a nursing home I'll still be thanking him. This rescue is my life."

Update: Jeanine's health has forced her to close The Cats Meow. As she slows down, volunteers are keeping Reuben's Room open at a reduced capacity. It's important to Jeanine to remain open to take back any cat she adopted out. "Once a Reuben's Room cat, always a Reuben's Room cat" is a commitment she plans on keeping.

Judy Austin with one of the cats in her rescue.

Every Cat has a Tale

In 2006, Judy Austin looked at her junk-filled garage and decided it was time for a change.

"It was too much space to waste," she said. She rented a Dumpster and filled it three times. Anything worth keeping was moved to an outbuilding on her Norton Shores property.

Judy's dream was to use the 24-by-26-foot garage for transitional housing for homeless cats. The new floor plan included an office, a laundry room and a large open space for free-roaming cats. Tinted windows, electrical outlets, and vents for heat and air-conditioning were installed, drywall nailed in place and a tile floor laid over the old cement.

I met Judy three years after the work on the garage was completed when I interviewed her for an article in *Cats and Dogs Magazine*.

Judy, now in her early 80s, has been rescuing cats and kittens for more years than she can remember—ever since her five children grew up and left home. She now has six grandchildren and nine great-grandchildren.

When she started, rescuing cats was a novel idea. "There were a lot of dog rescues, but no cat rescues. Cats were second class citizens," Judy explained. But she saw every cat as an individual and she considered them all first-rate citizens.

"Every cat has a story, but not every story is known," she said as she explained the meaning of the group's name—Cat Tales Rescue. The group is a non-profit 501(c)(3) organization.

The revamped garage is kitty-friendly. Cages are near windows so cats can watch wild birds flutter around seed-filled feeders and suspended suet cakes. One window provides access to an enclosed outside area. In warm weather, feline residents enjoy fresh country air, snooze in the sun and experience the aromas, sounds and sights of nature.

"They love it, and I love having it for them," Judy said.

While at the rescue, most cats are free-roaming. The only time they're confined to a cage is when they're new, sick or need a time-out for bad behavior. Cats climb and hide in the shelves used for the storage of canned food, bedding and other supplies. Scratching posts, toys and other amenities are plentiful. Residents also have the option of retreating to cages that have open doors.

Judy eventually transformed the office into a quarantine area and added an air purification system. The garage has room for 40 cats. A barn, that previous owners used to raise beagles, can house an additional 40 felines. The only time the rescue comes close to meeting its maximum quota is in spring and summer when babies are born.

"Kittens add up real fast," she said.

Judy said she has always had an attraction for animals. As a little girl she enticed cats and dogs to her home and told her mother they followed her.

In their heyday, it was common for Cat Tales Rescue to take in more than 300 cats annually. New homes were found through adoption events at PetSmart in Muskegon and online through Petfinder. Cat Tales is a no-kill sanctuary where cats stay until a perfect home is found.

Over the years numerous volunteers have helped Judy.

"They're very valuable to me," she said. "I could not do this alone. I love my volunteers." They help with cleaning, adoption events, running errands, giving the cats attention and anything else that needs doing.

Cat Tales is funded through donations, fundraising and adoption fees. The group holds bake sales and garage sales. Judy said she has applied for grants, but has never received one.

More than half of Cat Tales' budget goes to veterinarian care and medicines. Judy has learned how to do some medical care herself, including giving fluids and vaccines. "I learn quick when it saves money," she said.

Dr. Sara Prelesnik of Prelesnik Animal Hospital in Grand Haven is Cat Tales' primary veterinarian. "She's been very good to me. I couldn't do what I do without her," Judy said.

Judy's number one priority has always been getting her cats spayed and neutered. She would love to be put out of business, but doesn't think it's going to happen.

When I visited Judy in early 2022, she said she was ready to retire. A bout with Covid-19 and pneumonia had left her tired and feeling her age.

When she went to the hospital's emergency room when she wasn't feeling well, they wanted to admit her. She refused—she couldn't leave her cats unattended. So, home she went. For two months she didn't leave the house. Friends and volunteers brought her food and medicine and helped with the cats.

"I was one sick individual, but I beat it," she said, adding her doctor made house calls to check on her, and his wife and daughter came along and cleaned litter boxes and played with cats.

A month before she got sick, Judy celebrated her 80th birthday. A friend took her to a park in Muskegon to experience a zipline.

"I always wanted to do it. It was fun—scary too," she said. "I did it twice."

At the time of my visit, Judy had fewer than a dozen cats and had stopped intake. People continue to call and ask if she can take a cat or two, but as difficult as it is, she says no. "I can't go on forever. My volunteers are getting old too," she said. "I simply can't do it anymore. My heart is in it, but my body's not."

If she can't find homes for cats still in her care, they'll stay with her. "I'll never not have cats, but I need to make arrangements for them if something happens to me."

Sharon Lee with Sis, the mascot of Keeper Kitties.

Where Every Cat is a Keeper Kitty

Sharon Lee has always loved dogs and horses. She had cats, but to her they weren't the "be-all and end-all" in her life. She had no idea that those purring, furry felines would soon consume every aspect of her time.

The first time I saw Sharon, she was parading a foster dog around the West Michigan Pet Expo hoping to find the homeless pup a permanent home. My friends, Tricia and Mike McDonald, saw the lovable Jack Russell/Australian cattle dog and were smitten with the little guy and eventually adopted him.

When I learned Sharon had a cat rescue, I interviewed her for an article for my magazine, *Cats and Dogs Magazine.*

After being downsized out of a customer-service job in 2009, Sharon started volunteering at the Allegan County Animal Shelter, which was about 25 miles from her Wayland home. "I wanted to stay busy, and I always loved animals," she explained.

Walking dogs, cleaning cages and helping in the office turned into an education about homeless pets and animal rescue. One of her duties at the shelter was to decide which cats were to be euthanized. The shelter cages were always full, yet every day county residents dropped off more strays, unplanned litters and cats they no longer wanted. There were just too many cats, and shelter management believed the only solution was euthanasia.

"It broke my heart to see so many cats put down," Sharon said. "It was hell. It was painful."

In the midst of the tragedy, Sharon started appreciating cats. "Cats are funny, lovable. They all have personalities," she said.

Eventually, Wishbone Pet Rescue Alliance took over management of the county shelter. They brought with them the belief that euthanasia was not the solution to cat overpopulation. They advocated spay/neuter and held clinics for residents to bring in their cats for surgery. Wishbone also transferred cats and kittens to other shelters and to rescue groups to help relieve the overcrowding at the Allegan shelter.

Helping with one of those transfers, Sharon was supposed to deliver two litters of kittens to a shelter she had never visited before. She got lost, and in frustration gave up the search and brought the kittens to her home for the night.

"That started the whole thing," she recalled. She decided to keep the kittens and find them homes herself. She then started bringing more cats and kittens home.

64

"I have a good record at finding homes," she said.

She eventually resigned from the shelter. For a couple of years, Sharon volunteered wherever she was needed, including the Barry County Animal Shelter.

"Some incredible cats came into that shelter," she said. In 2013, she transported more than 350 cats from the Barry County shelter to rescue groups across the state.

Sharon was a member of Animal Rescues of Michigan and Imagine Home, a network of rescues that transports cats to rescues or shelters with extra space or places them in foster homes until they can be adopted.

When adoption fees and donations came up short to cover expenses related to Sharon's rescue work, she covered the costs out of her own pocket. A friend, who preferred to remain anonymous, suggested she become a non-profit. That friend had a foundation and could give her grants to help with expenditures if she was a registered non-profit organization.

"He's such a great animal lover. He has a heart of gold. I wouldn't be able to continue without his support," she said of her unnamed benefactor. In 2014 she followed his advice and founded her own rescue, Keeper Kitties Rescue, and became a 501(c)(3) non-profit organization.

Sharon operated the rescue out of her home, and she did everything—cleaning, feeding, trips to the vet, social media postings, updates on adoption sites and screening of applicants. Her sister, Pam Lee, helped when needed.

Where did the name Keeper Kitties come from?

Sharon explained that the name of the rescue

expressed her dream of the future: *Where every cat is a keeper kitty*. Where every cat has a loving home and there is no longer a need for euthanasia.

Keeper Kitties' mission was to find homeless cats their forever homes, to reduce overpopulation through education and the promotion of spay/neuter, and to act as a resource for pet services within the community.

Sharon said she developed an emotional attachment to every cat she took in and insisted on finding each one a perfect home—she required personal references, a veterinarian reference and she always did a home visit.

"I worry. I love every single one of them," she said.

She adopted out 50 to 70 cats per year.

The mascot of Keeper Kitties was Sis, a polydactyl, deaf white cat who came from a shelter. Sis sensed when a newcomer was frightened and befriended it.

"They gravitate to her when they're scared, and she builds confidence in them," Sharon explained.

Sharon finds homes for the cats through websites such as Petfinder and Adopt a Pet. She also takes cats to adoption days at area stores and to events such as Petapalooza and the West Michigan Pet Expo, which was where I first met her. In addition, she had a friend in Illinois who helped place cats.

Besides getting cats from overcrowded shelters, Sharon took in cats from the public. She's heard all the excuses people use for getting rid of a cat:

We're moving.

We have a new baby.

My boyfriend doesn't like cats.

The excuses make Sharon mad; she felt adopting a cat should be a life-long commitment, but if she had room she took the cat...and loved it.

Sharon transformed her home into a cat haven. To create separate spaces within the house, she installed Plexiglas doors at the kitchen entrance, the access point to the hallway and the doorway to the cat room.

While we talked in the living room, cats lounged on carpet covered trees in front of windows. Some spied on birds as they pecked at seeds in feeders. There were kennels for cats who weren't ready to roam free. A black kitten attacked my ink pen as I took notes.

The majority of the cats were in a room in the back of the house. They didn't all get along, so Sharon rotated them between free-roaming and caged. A lot of them were mom-cats whose babies had been adopted. Sharon called them the *leftovers*. A few were semi-feral and didn't like to be picked up. They would never be lap cats, which made them hard to place. Some will most likely stay with Sharon forever, but that's okay. She doesn't plan on getting out of rescue any time soon.

"I thought this was going to be temporary, but I don't know how to stop. It's become such a big part of my life and my heart," she said.

In 2018, Sharon had a series of small strokes that slowed her down. She lost her peripheral vision and decided it was no longer safe to drive. Her sister Pam, who lived with her, helped with the cats. The women are working at reducing the number of cats in their care. They're not taking in any more cats until Sharon's health stabilizes.

Sharon never thought she would be a crazy cat lady, but she's not offended by the title.

"My brother says, 'You can have as many cats as you want as long as you don't make the news.'"

Sharon never made the news, but she should have. The community needed to know of her compassion, her commitment and her love for cats.

Sharon's health eventually declined into dementia, and when Pam could no longer care for her at their home, she was admitted into a memory-care facility. Keeper Kitties was permanently closed, but hundreds of cats—maybe thousands—can thank Sharon for their chances of finding forever homes.

Janie Duca with her cats.

Miracles do Happen

In the early 2000s, a stray cat showed up at Janie Duca's Spring Lake home. She called the West Michigan SPCA (Society for the Prevention of Cruelty to Animals) and was told to bring them the cat. Janie was shocked by what she saw at their facility. "There were cats everywhere," she recalled. "I asked if they needed help."

They answered yes.

Janie has been a fan of cats for as long as she can remember and has always had at least one cat in her care. Friends and family give her cat-themed gifts, and her current obsession is collecting antique cat salt and pepper shakers.

Her license plate is CATGAGA.

"Yes, I'm definitely a crazy cat lady," she said.

Janie loves their independence, their fur and their smell. She thinks someone should make a man's cologne that captures the scent of cat. Any man who used it would attract women like catnip attracts felines.

When Janie started volunteering at the SPCA her first assignment was scrubbing cages. It didn't take her long to realize the cats weren't getting the attention they needed.

"I watched a lot of cats die," she said. Incoming cats weren't quarantined, sick cats weren't isolated and veterinarian care was rare.

The SPCA was housed on private property. Besides cats, there was a collection of hybrid wolves, exotic animals and even a few farm critters. The variety and number of animals proved to be disastrous as proper care couldn't be provided for all of them. Trouble ensued, and by court order all the animals, except the hybrid wolves, were relocated to sanctuaries and rescues. The cats were put into foster homes with the majority going to Janie's home.

"I'm surprised my husband is still with me," she said.

For two and half years, the Duca home provided a safe haven to numerous homeless cats. After putting in eight hours at her full-time job, Janie would come home and devote her free time to cleaning, feeding and doing whatever else was needed to take care of the cats.

"I don't know how I did it, but I did," she said, adding that other SPCA volunteers helped with the workload.

Officially the group was still West Michigan SPCA, but they started doing business as Faithful to Felines, a cats-only nonprofit rescue based in Muskegon.

I first met Janie at an adoption event at Petco. I'd see her at various events and came to know her as one of the core members of Faithful to Felines.

In 2010, the group started to look for their own facility. During their search, they found the perfect building. There was only one problem—at $399,000 the price was more than they could afford, but that didn't stop them from dreaming.

The five-acre site, at 2525 Hall Road in Muskegon, included two buildings. They envisioned using one for storage, the other to house cats. The one for cats had an atrium where kitties could spend time outdoors with no chance of escaping. A back hallway had doors to eight rooms. Each room had a large window overlooking woods and a double-doored closet with a sink and storage space. In their dream, each room housed a colony of kitties. The storage space filled with cat food, kitty litter and cleaning supplies.

"It was perfect," Janie said. But all she and the other volunteers could do was dream, because they couldn't afford it. Apparently, no one else could afford the building either, because it stayed on the market. Janie monitored the price, which continually dropped, but even at $199,000 it was still too much.

Then a miracle happened.

An attorney called and said a Muskegon woman with no family had included Faithful to Felines in her will and had left them close to $200,000. Everyone was speechless—no one in the group had ever met their benefactor, Casimar Paczosa.

After the shock wore off, Janie remembers thinking, *maybe we can get the building*. When the group received the money, they offered the building owner $100,000 cash—and it was accepted.

It took months to renovate the 4,000-square-foot building that would be used for the cats. Besides eight rooms for free-roaming cats, the facility had a large lobby and several offices that would be repurposed. Plans included an intake quarantine room, an area for sick cats, and a medical room where a veterinarian could treat cats and do spay/neuter surgeries. In addition, there was a kitchen, a laundry and bathrooms.

In April 2011, the work was completed and the cats were moved to their new quarters. The building has room for 100 cats. The second building was reserved for storage and special events.

Even with the bequest from Casimar Paczosa, the ongoing expense of having a facility and caring for close to 100 cats is daunting. Helping at a local bingo hall one night a week helps keep Faithful to Felines afloat.

"We wouldn't survive without it," Janie said.

The group also wouldn't survive without volunteers. About 40 people share the workload of cleaning, helping with adoptions, entertaining the cats, and anything else required to keep the shelter functioning.

An annual garage sale helps pay utilities, veterinarian bills and building upkeep. When there's a need it's posted on Facebook. "When we ask, people give," Janie said.

Janie has been volunteering for Faithful to Felines for 18 years. She has been on the board of directors since 2010 and has been the president for three years. She's also the facility director and puts in more than 30 hours every week.

Things have changed a lot since Janie's first days of volunteering at West Michigan SPCA.

"Cats seldom die here," she said. The group has a veterinarian on call, and Janie has learned a lot about the health care of cats and kittens.

They also have a room dedicated to FIV positive cats. FIV (feline immunodeficiency virus) affects a cat's immune system over a period of years. There was a time when infected cats were euthanized, but now they can often live long, healthy and relatively normal lives.

Janie has come to accept the fact that she can't help all the cats in need. While Faithful to Felines does a lot to help the cats of Muskegon County, Janie feels they barely put a dent in the problem. She's frustrated that the county doesn't give any financial aid for cats and that there are so many people who don't care.

At 62, Janie would like to slow down but said it's hard to do. Her back is bad and her shoulder hurts, but there are cats in need, so she keeps doing what needs to be done.

"I truly enjoy helping cats. It's very fulfilling," she said. "This is my niche in life."

For more information on Faithful to Felines, visit www.faithful2felines.com or follow them on Facebook.

Laura Moody with Larry right before he was adopted.

Giving Cats a Second Chance

When Laura Moody found herself unhappy as an x-ray technician and medical assistant, a friend shared an observation.

You love animals. You should dedicate your life to animals.

At the time, the Michigan native was living in Colorado. Heeding her friend's insight, Laura began volunteering for a cat rescue and was eventually hired as a caretaker. When she relocated to Grand Rapids, she volunteered at a local rescue and served as its vet tech.

"Those three and half years were good boot-camp training," she said.

In January 2021, Laura and a handful of like-minded friends started their own cat rescue. Their goal was to help abandoned cats and those in shelters at risk of being euthanized for behavioral issues.

The name they choose for the rescue, Second Chance Cats of West Michigan, fit their mission perfectly.

"Our focus is cats who are friendly, but scared or traumatized. Cats who need time to decompress and learn to trust again," Laura explained. "We want to give each one a second chance at a good home."

One such cat was Mouse, a shorthaired gray kitty who had been living in a colony in Grand Rapids. The stray was semi-friendly, obviously someone's pet at one time. He was live-trapped and neutered but became hissy and angry.

"He was so scared. Imagine having a home and then being put out on the street. You're trapped. Then you have surgery. Would you be friendly?" Laura asked.

But after eight months of hissing and hiding in his foster home, Mouse apparently realized he was in a safe, friendly place.

"He's now the sweetest cat in the world," Laura said, adding that a new home was found for Mouse.

What Laura loves about rescue is seeing a shy, scared cat, like Mouse, who doesn't trust humans, turn into a loving, trusting cat. She also loves hearing from people who have adopted and seeing the photos of the cats who are thriving after being given a second chance

"It's so rewarding," she said.

Second Chance Cats is a 501(c)(3) nonprofit organization. The first time I interviewed Laura, the group had just started renting space in a strip mall in Grand Rapids. She was excited and couldn't believe her dream of starting a rescue was really happening.

"It's awesome. Surreal," she said.

The suite has three rooms for free-roaming cats, a small lobby, a laundry, a bathroom and storage space. Since that first interview, Second Chance Cats started renting an additional suite next door, which gives them three more rooms. One is used for quarantine, one is an activity room and one is an event center where they can hold such things as yoga with cats.

Second Chance Cats' facility has room for up to 25 cats. Foster homes provide loving care for hospice cats and those in need of special care or socialization. Close to 70 volunteers keep the rescue purring along. All the cats they take in receive complete medical care, including spay/neuter surgery, vaccines, testing for feline diseases and anything else that is needed.

Second Chance Cats receives numerous emails requesting assistance. When they can't help, advice is offered.

"Rescues aren't the only ones who can help. Everyone can help," Laura explained. She would love for people who find a stray to keep it in their garage or bathroom for a few days or a week until space is available, and to look for the cat's owners. Rescues are usually full, especially during kitten season, and any help people can provide is welcomed.

"We're all in this together," she said. "There are too many cats. Spay and neuter your pets, please."

For Laura, seeing neglected and abandoned cats is a difficult facet of rescue. One such cat was a Siamese left outside when her owners moved from an apartment complex. She was skinny and covered with fleas, which caused anemia.

"Abandonment is never the answer," Laura said.

Esme, as she was named, was taken to a vet where it was discovered she had a blood parasite. A couple days later, Esme was drooling, not eating and seemed to have trouble breathing. She was then taken to an emergency hospital, but they couldn't determine what was going on. They prescribed pain meds and an appetite stimulant. Esme ate for a couple days, then quit. It was discovered her tongue was ulcerated, which led to the diagnose of calicivirus, a contagious virus that causes a mild upper respiratory infection and oral disease in cats. Pain meds were again prescribed, and Esme was placed in a foster home to recuperate.

"She's definitely in a lot of pain, but she's on the road to recovery," Laura said.

An online fundraiser for $1,500 was started to cover the veterinarian expenses for Esme. It didn't take long for the group's followers to donate what was needed. Second Chance Cats is funded primarily through community donations.

Laura said there's a vaccine for calicivirus and urges people to have their cats vaccinated. Esme hadn't been vaccinated nor was she spayed.

Ever since she was a little girl, Laura has had a passion for animals. "I just love helping animals," she said.

Laura was a dog person until her boyfriend, Ryan (now her husband) surprised her with a kitten he and some friends had found. The kitten, a patch tabby they named Leo, lived to be 17 and just recently passed.

"Ryan got me to love cats," she admitted. Little did she know where that love of cats would lead her. "Having a rescue is not all sunshine and rainbows. There are a lot of tough things, but it's my passion. It's worth it."

For more information visit www.sccatswm.org. Follow them on Facebook: Second Chance Cats of WM or Instagram: @sccatswm.

Wendee Hofbauer with Loki, her newest foster fail.

A Palace for Piper

When her four-year-old cat died in early 2019, Wendee Hofbauer was devastated. She had adopted Piper as a kitten and had fallen in love with the gray and white kitty.

"I had her four short years," she said. A string Piper had eaten punctured her intestines; the damage couldn't be repaired.

To honor Piper, Wendee started a kitten rescue in her hometown of Zeeland. Piper's Palace, a foster-based nonprofit, opened in July 2019. The original intent was to rescue kittens, but that mission didn't last long. Wendee hadn't anticipated the requests from people to take nursing moms and pregnant cats—and she couldn't say no. She also can't say no to rabbits, lizards, hedgehogs and other small pets—fortunately those requests are few. Nowadays the majority of the cats and kittens in Piper's adoption program come in as strays or owner surrenders.

Wendee's initiation into rescue began as a volunteer at a local humane society where she fell in love with all the animals. "My love of animals is nothing I have felt before. Yes, I have family and friends who love me, but they also judge me, and animals don't," she said.

In the three years since Piper's Palace was founded, Wendee has found new homes for close to 450 cats and kittens. Not bad for a group that operates with a skeleton crew. Besides Wendee, there are only four volunteers who foster. Her fiancé, who serves as the group's president, also helps where he can.

For Wendee, finding that perfect home for a cat or kitten is the best part of rescue—knowing that a pet gets to live its best life. She loves updates on adopted fosters.

The hardest thing about running a rescue is the finances. "I thought it would be easier," Wendee admitted. The group is funded primarily through community donations, but veterinarian bills come in faster than the charitable contributions.

Wendee pays for expenses when donations aren't enough. She works 40-50 hours a week at a Holland-based company. "If I didn't work, Piper's Palace wouldn't be here," she said.

Volunteers help with the group's annual fundraiser— this year the event is named Kitties and Costumes. The Halloween-themed party will have a silent auction, costume contest, a photo booth and a DJ. Proceeds go toward the group's future shelter, aka the Palace. Plans for the Palace include rooms for free-roaming cats, an area for sick cats, space for adoption visits, a veterinarian room where spay/neuter surgeries can be performed and a wing for feral cats. The Palace will be built in stages as funds become available.

Piper's Palace partners with PetSmart in Holland where they do adoptions the first weekend of each month. All their cats and kittens are vet checked, spayed/neutered, microchipped, have age-appropriate vaccines, are treated for fleas/ticks and are dewormed.

Wendee said there are times she feels like quitting, especially when she knows the stray cat population is out of control and what she does is almost insignificant. She gets frustrated when people get a free pet and then use it for breeding or treat it like trash.

"They have feelings and a heartbeat, just like you and I," she said.

For more information on Piper's Palace, visit www.piperspalace.org or follow them on Facebook.

Nancy Mogle with one of the cats in Vicky's Pet
Connection's adoption program.

Tenacity and Energy

One summer evening in 1997, Nancy Mogle and Vicky Freund stared into the flames of a campfire and had a heartfelt conversation about animal rescue. The women, both volunteers at the Kent County Humane Society, were dissatisfied with several aspects of their charitable work.

That night they made a life-altering decision—they were going to start an animal rescue.

"Vicky is a dreamer and I'm an organizer," Nancy explained. Vicky's dream of the women venturing out on their own was the beginning of Vicky's Pet Connection, the first animal rescue in West Michigan. Nancy's organizational skills propelled the group through more than two decades of rescue.

Another difference between the two women was their preference in pets. Vicky favored dogs while Nancy preferred cats.

I first met Nancy more than 30 years ago when we both volunteered at Ottawa County Humane Society, now known as Harbor Humane Society. We were part of a fundraising team that put piggy banks in local businesses. Every month we collected the donated change, counted it and turned the money into the shelter. Nancy and I hadn't kept in touch. I didn't see her again until I was gathering information for an article about Vicky's Pet Connection for *Cats and Dogs Magazine*. I was stunned to learn Nancy was the co-founder of the pioneering rescue.

Nancy can no longer recall the issues that drove a number of people to leave the humane society, now the Humane Society of West Michigan. She does admit she has a bad habit of wanting control, of not following protocols, and overstepping boundaries, but for her the reasons no longer matter.

"Vicky's was born out of conflict, but our hallmark today is collaboration," she said.

West Michigan's cats and dogs were the winners when that handful of discontents walked away from the humane society. Out of dissatisfaction, two organizations were created that have had a lasting impact on the pet population in our area.

While Vicky and Nancy started Vicky's Pet Connection to find homes for cats and dogs rescued from shelters, other disgruntled volunteers started C-SNIP, a low-cost spay/neuter clinic in Grand Rapids. C-SNIP has performed thousands of surgeries, thus preventing the birth of countless litters of puppies and kittens.

When the women started Vicky's Pet Connection, both the Kent County Animal Shelter and the humane society refused to release animals to them. "We had to earn our stripes," Nancy said.

The Ionia County Animal Shelter was the only local shelter that allowed Vicky's to pull cats and dogs. Nancy reminisced about the first two cats Vicky brought home from Ionia. They named them Thelma and Louise, and both were pregnant.

"Thelma and Louise were Vicky's way of sucking me in," said Nancy, who at that point hadn't yet fully committed to rescue, but Thelma and Louise changed her mind.

One of the moms-to-be gave birth to a single gray kitten, which the women found by itself in the middle of the room where the two cats were housed. Neither cat would take care of the baby. Both cats, along with the kitten, were taken to a veterinarian, but the vet couldn't determine which cat had given birth.

"Nobody wanted him. He was an outsider," Nancy said.

They named the baby Doogie after the medical prodigy Dr. Douglas "Doogie" Howser in the 1989-93 TV comedy-drama.

A couple days after Doogie was born, each cat gave birth and together they had ten additional kittens, all of them black.

For Nancy, Doogie was a lesson in cat reproduction; a female cat can mate with more than one male. Doogie must have been conceived a few days before his littermates and therefore born before they were.

"It fascinated me. That's when I became a cat lady," Nancy said.

Looking back, Nancy is amazed Doogie survived. At the time she didn't have any experience in taking care of a newborn kitten, but caring for the rejected baby created a bond and Nancy adopted Doogie.

When the Kent County Animal Shelter continued to refuse to release animals to Vicky's, Nancy started volunteering for the shelter. The doors gradually opened.

"That forged a partnership that exists to this day," Nancy said.

A weekly morning ritual began. For 15 years, Nancy went to the shelter every Monday to select cats for their adoption program. On average, she would take 30 to 35 cats—the number was dependent on how much space she had in their cattery and foster homes.

The shelter was always full. Nancy knew the cats she didn't take would be gone the following Monday—most likely victims of euthanasia, not adoption.

In their heyday, Vicky and Nancy pulled close to 1,300 animals from the shelter every year. Seventy-five percent of those were cats.

The women turned the basement of their Ada home into a cattery and built a kennel in their yard for dogs.

"With energy and tenacity, you can get a lot done," said Nancy who described herself as having a Type A personality.

According to the *New Oxford American Dictionary, Type A individuals are outgoing, ambitious, rigidly organized, sensitive, impatient, anxious, proactive, and concerned with time management. They are often high-achieving workaholics.*

The description fits Nancy like a glove.

Eventually, Vicky's Pet Connection opened the Critter Cottage in Ada. The cottage sells pet-related items, has two rooms for free-roaming adoptable cats and provides space for meet-and-greet of dogs in foster care.

When I interviewed Nancy in 2018, she was getting about 300 cats per year from the county shelter.

"We are so blessed," Nancy said, adding Vicky and she both had good jobs and were gifted with energy. They were also fortunate to have support from animal-loving community leaders, even when the local animal shelters didn't quite trust the newly founded rescue.

While Nancy is retired from her day job, she still puts in more than ten hours every day taking care of cats, handling adoptions, dealing with emails, phone calls, and office work. "I always have a battle in my soul to balance work and play," she said. Her problem is she considers working with cats as play. "I'm looking for moderation."

Now in her early 70s, Nancy said she is slowing down and notices a decrease in mental agility, but she acknowledges there are still cats and kittens in need.

"Cats are so disposable," she said, adding that it's all about supply and demand. If there were fewer cats, they would increase in value.

While Nancy still devotes her days to cats, she tries to be done by 4:30 p.m. when Vicky gets home from work.

The women have been together 29 years and keep each other in check regarding their number of pets. Currently they have four dogs and four cats.

"I'm the happiest person you'll ever meet," Nancy claims. "I have a contentment in life I never knew was possible and it's because of cats. They give a Zen calmness. They purr, it's the best sound. When a shy cat kisses you it's an indescribable place of joy."

Update: Nancy and Vicky decided to close Vicky's Pet Connection starting Jan. 1 2021. During their 23 years of rescue, the group found homes for more than 16,000 cats and dogs. They also provided spay/neuter surgeries for almost 20,000 animals. They feel comfortable leaving rescue to the next generation of animal lovers.

Diane Valk with kittens available for adoption at
Heaven Can Wait's Resale Store.

What Can We Do?

In 2007, three women drove from Muskegon to Chicago to attend a PetSmart Charities no-kill conference. The women wanted to learn what they could do to help homeless animals.

"We wanted to learn anything and everything about spay and neuter," said Lisa Westerburg, who made the drive with Diane Valk and Rita Theeuwes.

At the conference, Diane remembers saying to one of the conference organizers, "We're moms. We're animal lovers. What can we do?"

Diane learned that the overpopulation problem, and subsequent euthanasia, was due to the lack of accessible, low-cost spay and neuter services. There was a low-cost spay/neuter clinic 35 miles from Muskegon, so the best thing the women could do was transport animals to get them fixed.

The clinic the organizer referred to was C-SNIP, on the south side of Grand Rapids in Kentwood. The long distance made it impossible for working families in Muskegon County to use the clinic's services.

The advice resonated with the women. "We were so inspired. The drive back is where we decided to start Heaven Can Wait," Diane said.

Back at home, the women did the paperwork for Heaven Can Wait Animal Haven to become a nonprofit. They contacted C-SNIP about their plans. When the details were worked out, they ran an ad in the Muskegon Chronicle offering the transport service. Pet owners had to pay the spay/neuter fee plus a $10 donation that would be used to help those who couldn't afford the cost.

The women shared the workload. Lisa handled incoming calls for transport, scheduling and all the paperwork that accompanied each transport.

"My phone rang off the hook," she said.

Diane and Lisa used their own vehicles to make the drive to C-SNIP and paid for their own gas.

On Thursdays before work, Diane, who managed her husband's dental practice, would meet people in various parking lots. She'd collect the fees, load the animals and then make the drive to C-SNIP. On Friday morning she'd reverse the operation—pick up the animals, return to the parking lots and wait for the owners to claim their pets.

Rita assisted the transports. In the early mornings, she greeted people in the parking lots and helped get pets loaded. She'd go to a full-time job and then return to help unload pets and give owners discharge information.

Lisa said they logged hundreds of hours in the rain,

heat and snow. Other volunteers joined the cause and helped with phone calls, scheduling, paperwork for the transports and driving.

On one of the return trips, a woman who had brought a mom-cat and six black kittens told Diane she didn't want the kittens back. Diane recalls looking at the adorable babies and thinking, *now what?* She called Lisa, and Lisa told her to take them.

Lisa had an idea. She called the local Petco and asked if they could bring the kittens to the store on the weekend to find them homes. That was the beginning of a relationship with Petco that exists to this day. It also was the beginning of Heaven Can Wait expanding their services to include rescue, foster and adoptions.

It wasn't long before they began going to the Muskegon County Animal Shelter, which was managed by Pound Buddies Rescue, and pulling cats and placing them into foster homes.

"It seemed perfectly logical to use our own homes as mini-shelters to buy them the time they needed to eventually get adopted," Lisa explained.

The first time Diane went to the shelter to look at cats, 19 were tagged for euthanasia. "I was crying. I was mad at the world for doing this to cats," she said. She took all of them—and all of them had upper respiratory infections. They were taken to the vet and put on meds. When the cats were healthy and spayed/neutered, they were put up for adoption. Diane still remembers the first shelter cat to get adopted—Superman, a big orange tomcat.

Doing adoptions at Petco on Saturdays became a regular event. Then they added Sundays. Then Fridays.

Heaven Can Wait transported 80 to 100 cats and dogs every month. Pound Buddies Rescue eventually took over transporting dogs, and Heaven Can Wait dedicated their resources to cats.

Heaven Can Wait also gets involved in rescue situations that involve significant numbers of unattended and neglected cats. In October 2013, they were notified by animal control that 25 cats were living in a mobile home in hoarding conditions. The total actually turned out to be 92 cats. They've dealt with several cases with similar number of cats.

Rita was the accountant for the group, but also helped with transport and fostering. When Rita remarried and moved out of state, her involvement with the group ended.

Lisa moved to New Buffalo in 2009. Then to California. She now lives in Minnesota. Despite the moves, Lisa continues to help with record keeping and grant writing. Due to health issues, her involvement is now limited, although she remains a board member.

"I stay involved because Heaven Can Wait is near and dear to my heart, and I want to help in any way that I can," Lisa said. Lisa loves all animals and has been a vegetarian for more than 30 years.

Lisa said they have transported well over 7,000 animals for spay/neuter surgeries. Volunteers continue to transport, but the cats are now taken to Quick Fix Veterinary Clinic in Alto.

When I interviewed Diane in May 2022, the group had 227 volunteers and close to 500 cats in foster homes. They expect to adopt out more than 2,000 cats and kittens in 2022.

"It's truly remarkable and impressive," Diane said of the group's accomplishments.

She told a story of her husband taking her out to dinner on a Saturday night. On the drive to Grand Rapids, she received a phone call about an injured stray cat. She called a volunteer and asked if the woman could pick up the cat and take it to a vet. The answer was yes. Then she called another volunteer and asked if she could foster the cat after the veterinarian finished the exam. Again, the answer was yes.

Her husband, who overheard the conversations, asked her if anyone ever told her no. His question took Diane by surprise, but after thinking about it for a moment she answered no.

Volunteers are always ready to drop what they are doing to help a cat in need.

"We have the best volunteers. It's why I can do what I do—because of everyone else. What our volunteers do is indescribable," Diane said.

Heaven Can Wait has several streams of revenue. The group receives grants from the Petco Love and Bissell Pet Foundation. They have a resale store where all the items are donated and all the workers are volunteers.

In 2018, they started collecting returnable cans and bottles that volunteers return to area stores. The returnables have netted them more than $100,000. The Covid-19 shutdown, when stores weren't accepting cans and bottles, played a big part in reaching the $100,000 milestone. The group stockpiled donated returnables until stores restarted their bottle return operations. The empty bottles and cans continue to be lucrative. "It has exceeded our wildest dreams and brings in more than $2,000 per month," Lisa said.

Several times a year the group holds bake sales. The sales have become so popular that people line up to purchase the homemade treats.

"Our community is amazing. They adopt. They donate. They shop. It truly takes a village," Diane said.

Muskegon County is now no-kill when it comes to cats, which means no adoptable cats or kittens are euthanized. Diane's advice to those who want to help cats is to start in their own community.

"When it's no-kill, reach out beyond your community. That's how we'll become a no-kill nation," she said.

Fifteen years after that fateful trip to the no-kill conference in Chicago, Diane still loves being involved in rescue. "You have to be passionate. You have to be dedicated and you have to love it—I'm proud to be part of it," she said.

For more information on Heaven Can Wait Animal Haven visit www.heavencanwaitmi.org or follow them on Facebook.

Hannah Rae Hilborn with one of her foster kittens.

Making it Official

Hannah Rae Hilborn lives in Muskegon Heights and sees first-hand the need for more people to get involved in cat rescue. "There's a lot of evictions here and a lot of cats are left behind when people move," she said.

Hannah does what she can to help homeless cats including TNR. But most of the cats she traps are friendly and can't be returned to where they were caught, because they're house cats and can't survive on their own. She has the cats scanned for microchips and occasionally finds one, but so far, no owners have responded to calls.

She brings the abandoned cats to Faithful to Felines, where she volunteers, but she said she doesn't want to continue to burden them with so many cats.

A friend suggested she start her own rescue.

"I never thought of making it official," she said.

In March 2022, she took the plunge and applied to become a 501(c)(3) organization. The nonprofit status was granted in May.

She named the foster-based rescue Grimalkin's Rescue—Grimalkin is an archaic term for cat.

Hannah also started a Facebook page and created a website for the rescue. Her mission is to help reduce the population of unwanted and uncared for cats by providing spay/neuter, foster homes and adoptions. She also has a pet food pantry for those in need in hopes of keeping more pets and families together.

"The support has been incredible," she said.

She has received donations of food, litter boxes, cages, blankets and more. Some supplies even came from established rescues who had extra items.

Hannah currently has seven foster cats at her home. When I visited two feral kittens shared a playpen in the dining room where they could become accustomed to people. Hannah has two young children. The family has a dog and four cats of their own. The busy household helps socialize the hissy kittens, who, after just a week, were starting to become tame.

Hannah grew up on a farm with working cats. "That's where the love came from," she said. She is a magnet to stray animals. Wherever she has lived, she has opened her heart and doors to animals in need of help.

One of Hannah's goals for the rescue is to help with the overpopulation of cats. "A big part of that is helping educate people," she said. She added there are people who feed stray cats but don't get them spayed or neutered. "They have good hearts but they're contributing to the problem—they're creating breeding grounds."

Hannah regularly sees dead cats who have been hit and killed by cars. For her, they are a constant reminder of the overpopulation of cats in Muskegon.

Hannah has a passion for all animals. When she saw a Facebook post about the City of Muskegon selling land to Northern Biomedical Research (NBR), a company that uses animals in its research, she got involved. She started a Facebook group to connect with like-minded people.

"It blew up and became an unintended project. I became an accidental group leader," she said. Hannah spoke at city commission meetings and encouraged others to do the same. She also helped organize demonstrations. The group had two billboards to inform people of the issue. Unfortunately, the county approved the sale of the land and a tax abatement for NBR.

A few months after opening Grimalkin's Rescue, Hannah said she already has a waitlist and receives calls daily asking for help with cats.

She added that being is rescue can be overwhelming at times, but it can also be rewarding, especially when a cat or kitten gets adopted.

"That's what it's all about," she said.

For more information on Grimalkin's Rescue, visit grimalkinrescue.wordpress.com or follow the group's Facebook page.

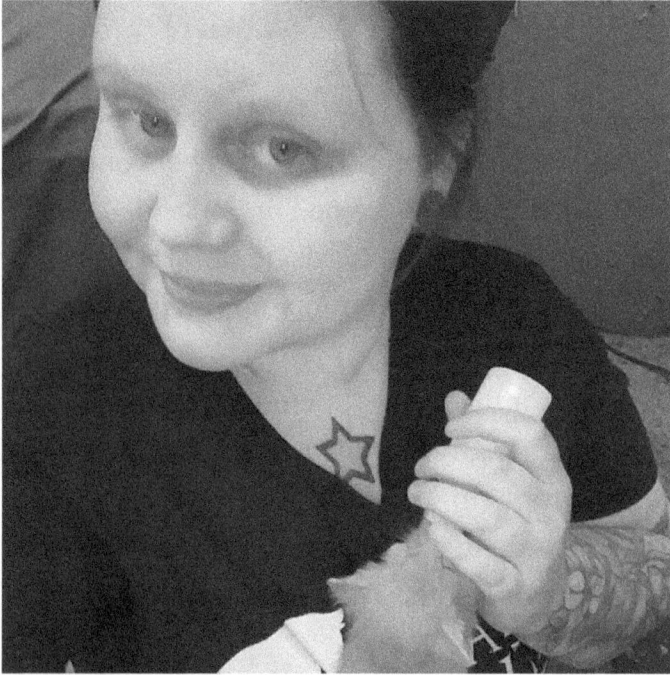
Chalsey Schmidt bottle feeding a kitten.

Kittens and More

Chalsey Schmidt's journey in rescuing cats started when she was eight years old. She found a kitten, and her mother taught her how to bottle-feed the youngster. "I was in love," she recalled. She named the tiny baby Ashes.

If anyone asked Chalsey what she wanted to do when she grew up, she told them she wanted to rescue cats. And that's exactly what she's doing. Through word-of-mouth she became the go-to person when orphan kittens were found. So, far she has bottle-fed more than 250 kittens.

"It's tiring. It's exhausting, but I can't see my life without kittens," Chalsey said.

Newborn kittens have to be fed every two hours. Every week the time between feedings can be increased by an hour.

Chalsey admits letting her bottle-fed kittens be adopted is hard, but she's cautious when approving adoptions. "I make sure they go to the best possible home," she said. She loves it when adopters send her photographs. "It's not required, but I always ask if they can send pictures."

For a time Chalsey had a small rescue, Halo's Helping Paws. Then she started volunteering for other groups including Pipers Palace in Zeeland.

In 2021, Chalsey decided to venture out on her own and founded Kittens in the Mittens, a nonprofit, 501(c)(3) organization that relies solely on donations and volunteers.

"This is what I was meant to do," Chalsey said. Besides, her mother, her husband (The Cat Man) and their two young children help. "My daughter is a little cat lady." They have taken in more than 475 cats. Close to half of them have been adopted. She has several foster families including her parents.

The name of the group—Kittens in the Mittens—is deceiving. While the group works with kittens, they also help adult cats, including ferals, through TNR.

One of the reasons Chalsey wanted to start her own rescue was to expand beyond kittens. "I want to do more with special-needs cats," Chalsey explained. "I like the difficult cases that other rescues don't want to take on."

Special-needs cats require extra care and can incur higher veterinarian expenses. Finding them homes can take more time too. "You need to find that special person for them," she explained.

Chalsey has taken in a blind cat, a cat who was shot and had bleach dumped on her and a cat with a broken jaw. One of the special-needs kittens the group took in is

Marmie, a black little bundle of energy and love. A woman contacted Chalsey about a newborn who wasn't acting right. The kitten came from a large litter and it was determined her back legs and tail had been paralyzed invitro. Chalsey took the kitten, which had to be bottle-fed.

"She's buff," Chalsey said. At five months, Marmie drags herself around and can climb most anything.

Chalsey also takes in CH kittens. CH—cerebellar hypoplasia—is sometimes called wobbly cat syndrome. It's a congenital condition that isn't contagious nor progressive. It occurs most commonly when a pregnant cat becomes infected with feline panleukopenia virus and passes it to her unborn kittens.

CH affects the cerebellum of the kittens, which is the area of the brain that controls fine motor movement, balance and coordination. The affected cats often have noticeable symptoms from birth, which range from mild signs of head bobbing and high stepping to more severe signs like tremors and the inability to walk. Symptoms may vary greatly between littermates.

Cats and kittens with CH can lead normal, happy, and healthy lives. It does not affect their life expectancy and many adapt exceedingly well to their disability. They often need extra traction, such as mats or carpet, to help them maneuver around. Cats and kittens should not be declawed as they rely on their claws for stability and balance.

When we talked, Kittens in the Mittens had two litters of CH kittens.

Chalsey recently took in two 12-year-old cats, Cuddles and Fluffies, whose elderly owner had died. They had been abandoned in the woman's house for a month—her son was going to have them euthanized.

Chalsey takes in cats from all over the state, but gets quite a few from around Flint and Detroit. She recently took in ten orange cats from a hoarding case in Livonia—an elderly man collected orange cats and had close to 40 identical-looking cats in his care. Not one cat was spayed or neutered.

"It was completely out of control," Chalsey said of the Orange Cat Hoarding Case. She regretted they could only take ten, but she didn't have foster homes for more than that ten.

Veterinarian care is Chalsey's biggest expense. She uses Hamilton Veterinary Clinic. "They're my life saver," she said. Every cat she takes in gets a checkup at the clinic. They also get spayed or neutered, vaccinated and microchipped.

Kittens in the Mitten is funded through adoption fees, donations and "our own pockets." They have a donation barrel at the Holland Pet Supplies Store.

Chalsey caught Covid-19 and was quite sick but couldn't rest for long. "I'm tired, but there's such an over population of cats—we have to do more," she said. "No one should be breeding cats when they can get a perfect cat off the street."

For more information visit www.kittensinthemitten.org.

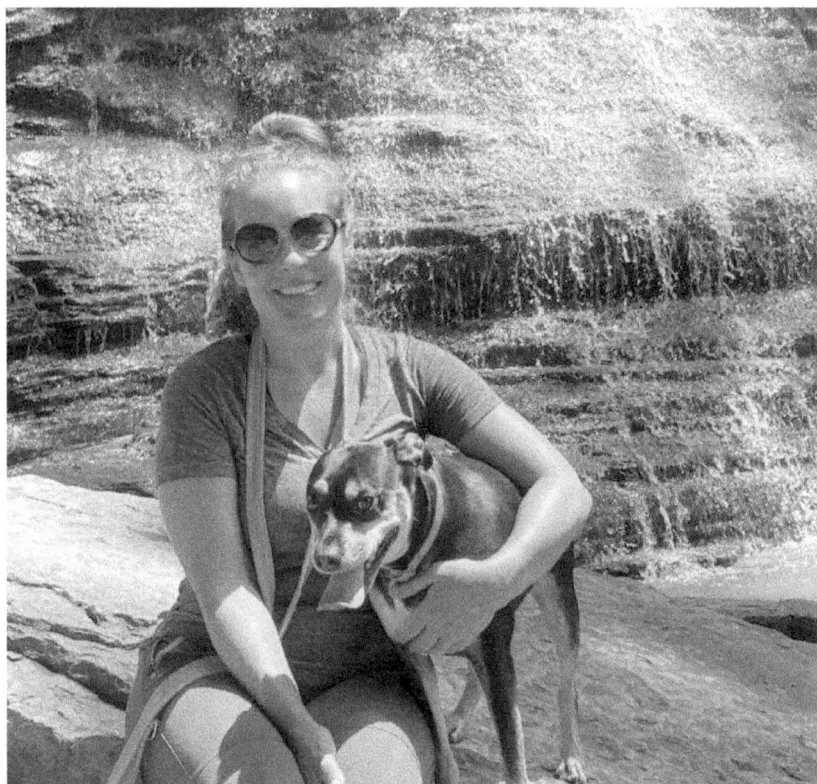

Gina Marvin and Karma, who she adopted from the
Kent County Animal Shelter.

Feral Cat Champion

In 2005, Gina Marvin was a mail carrier in a low-income neighborhood in Grand Rapids. As she walked her route, she noticed outside cats—they were everywhere.

"If not for my job, I wouldn't have seen it," she said. "It was glaring in my face."

Seeing the cats changed her life.

Gina went online to find help. She discovered there weren't any local groups geared towards helping feral cats. She also learned if such a cat was taken to the local animal shelter it was routinely euthanized.

"It's inhumane; they have a right to life," she said.

Feral cats are sometimes referred to as community cats. They're not socialized to people but are part of the community. The outdoors is their home.

Online Gina stumbled upon Alley Cat Allies, a national non-profit organization that advocates for feral cats. Alley Cat endorses trap-neuter-return (TNR) as the most humane and effective method to reduce feral cat populations. In TNR, feral cats are live-trapped, spayed or neutered and returned to where they were caught. While anesthetized, the cat is ear-tipped, which is an indication a feral cat is fixed. The procedure involves removing a quarter-inch off the tip of a cat's left ear.

Gina bought a live trap and was fortunate to have Dr. Wendy Swift, who worked at the Humane Society of West Michigan, agree to do spay/neuter surgeries on the cats she trapped. She then knocked on doors of the homes where she saw numerous cats and asked if she could help.

"People were leery," Gina recalled. But after she explained she would live-trap the cats, get them fixed and bring them back, people accepted her help. "It quickly went from me seeking out cats to people being referred to me."

When she first started trapping cats, Gina paid for the surgeries herself but that soon changed. "I realized I could reach more cats by starting a nonprofit than continuing to work as an individual and paying for everything myself," she said.

Gina founded Focus on Ferals. Its mission was TNR.

Gina never intended to do adoptions, but she couldn't ignore the numerous kittens and friendly strays she came across. There were too many to take to the animal shelter or humane society. So, adoptions became part of the group's mission.

The next addition to her undertaking was helping county animal shelters. Early in her rescue career, Gina pulled a few cats from a local shelter. "I realized some cats shut down and are terrified in a traditional shelter setting," she explained. Word got around, and staff at county shelters started asking her for help when they were at capacity or had cats who were struggling.

"Our shelter program was never part of the original rescue plan, but we're able to help cats who wouldn't have made it out alive," she said.

Despite all the add-on activities, Focus on Ferals continues to do TNR, but the service isn't advertised. Referrals from prior clients and other organizations keep volunteers busy. The group also supplies cat food to people who care for colonies of spayed/neutered feral cats. In addition, they provide winter shelters and medical care when needed.

"It's a huge weight. There's a huge number of people who rely on us," Gina said.

In 2014, the group moved into a 2,600-square-foot building in Byron Center.

"We finally had a facility which reflected our compassion for and commitment to every cat that passes through our doors," Gina said.

Their prior location in northeast Grand Rapids had been used for adoptable cats while Gina's Lowell home was used for TNR services. With it out of her house, she could decompress when she went home.

The new place was five times larger and had five rooms for free-roaming cats available for adoption. There was a lobby, an office, a bathroom (which the old facility didn't have) and a large garage area with a washer and dryer and space for cats waiting to see the vet or recovering from surgery.

In the 17 years since Focus on Ferals was started, the group has trapped more than 3,000 cats and adopted out more than 4,000 cats. The group has close to 150 volunteers including people who foster. They receive a lot of community support.

"I truly believe that when your heart is true, people can see it, and they are inspired to help. Our community has shown us through their financial support, that they believe in our mission, and they trust in our ability to care for these cats," Gina said.

Animal rescue has a high burnout rate, and Gina has been rescuing cats for 17 years. I asked about her longevity.

"You have to be self-aware," she explained.

It took Gina several years to learn she needed to take a break when she felt stressed. Now when she feels the pressure of demanding circumstances, she goes hiking or spends a day at the beach. She also takes vacations—multi-day road trips out-of-state. She's thankful volunteers can manage the shelter when she needs to decompress.

Gina has also learned which aspects of rescue gives her joy and which ones don't. She loves hands-on caring for cats, managing the TNR program, and deciding which cats will enter their adoption program.

She doesn't like managing people or doing adoptions. "Those things drain me. I'm actually a super introvert. I require a lot of time alone," she explained.

There are volunteers who enjoy doing the things Gina finds draining.

While Focus on Ferals has expanded into adoptions and pulling cats from shelters, its primary focus remains spaying and neutering feral cats. "It's not glamorous or warm and fuzzy," Gina said. "I wish feral cats weren't the lowest man on the totem pole in the cat world."

She said it's a myth that feral cats lead miserable lives. "They're happy cats, definitely worthy of the resources we're putting into them." She added that the first colonies of cats that they TNR'd in 2005 either have no cats or just one or two left, which proves the effectiveness of TNR.

"It's the most humane solution," she said.

As a child, Gina didn't have any pets. She didn't get her first cat until she was 22 years old. Despite her slow start, Gina's passion for cats can't be denied. "This is what I've been called to do with my life," she said.

For more information on Focus on Ferals follow them on Facebook or Instagram or visit www.focusonferals.org.

Nicole McAndrew and Ivy.

Kitty Calling

When Nicole McAndrew was young, her grandparents had an auto junkyard down the road from where she lived. Numerous cats made their home among the rusted heaps of discarded vehicles. Unfortunately, predators, traffic and disease took a toll on the cats, sometimes leaving behind kittens. As a child, Nicole taught herself to mimic the meows of a mom-cat to lure orphans from their hiding places. If needed, her grandmother would bottle feed the motherless kittens.

Kitty calling—as Nicole refers to it—is a talent she has perfected and uses in cat rescue. She can imitate a female cat in heat to attract males or impersonate kittens to persuade mom-cats to enter live traps. And when needed, Nicole can still convince kittens to come out of hiding.

Nicole makes recordings of her calls for friends to use when they're trying to catch a cunning cat. She recommends covering a live-trap with a blanket and placing a Bluetooth speaker on top of it.

"She's amazing. Cats perk up when they hear her. It's magic," Thalia Ambriz said.

Thalia, a board member and foster for Nicole's ever-growing cat rescue, specializes in caring for neonate kittens. She's also a licensed wildlife rehabilitator.

Camilla Lamer is also a board member and foster. She has a quarantine room in her basement so cats and kittens can be deemed healthy before going to foster homes.

"Most fosters want healthy cats," Nicole explained.

The women focus on rescuing homeless and abandoned cats and kittens. "Nicole is the best. She'll go to any extreme to catch these cats," Thalia said.

Nicole's involvement in rescue began in 2015 when she and her husband, Chris, started to help friends look for lost dogs. They started Furry Friends Pet Recovery while helping catch a three-year-old dachshund, named June, who was on the run in Zeeland. They followed online pet recovery courses, established feeding stations and bought live traps. After 138 days, June was finally caught.

By word-of-mouth, it got out that Nicole and her friends helped catch missing pets. Soon she was tagged on social media posts regarding lost pets. Using trail cameras, search parties, flyers, live-traps and more, Nicole and her friends have helped catch cats, dogs and injured wildlife.

When Nicole was asked to help catch feral kittens in Burnips, she used her cat calls to convince nine kittens and their mom to come out from under a trailer.

"When they came out, I'd grab them," she said.

While Nicole continues to help catch lost and injured

animals, she's drawn to helping cats. "Basically, my heart is for the ferals and shy kitties," she said. She runs a rehabilitation program at her home for cats and kittens in need of socialization. Nicole also has a soft spot for special-needs kittens and cats.

Nicole receives an endless number of calls, texts and pleas for help. Our interview was postponed several times due to Nicole having a change of plans because she needed to rescue or transport cats or kittens.

Last August, Nicole and her friends helped with a hoarding case in Allegan that involved 64 cats. One neighbor was catching kittens and drowning them, and another neighbor was using kittens for target practice.

Thalia explained that during the Covid-19 shutdown, veterinarians were only allowed to provide essential services. Unfortunately, spay and neuter surgeries weren't considered essential.

"The cat population has exploded," she said.

Another part of the problem is how cats are perceived, especially in rural areas—they're seen as disposable, a nuisance and are often unwanted. "We need to change the culture of how we look at cats," Thalia explained. Their goals include educating people about trap-neuter-return and spay/neuter.

"But we can't do it alone. We need more fosters and more veterinarians," Nicole said. They have 67 cats and kittens in foster homes.

Nicole is a hairstylist, a "manipulator of hair" and an artist in hair coloring. She was voted #1 in the Holland

Sentinel's Best of the Best contest eight years in a row.

While the women pay some of the expenses associated with rescuing cats and kittens out-of-pocket, help comes from social media requests, bake sales, raffles and an Amazon wish list. Private donors, friends and family members also contribute.

Nicole's heart was stolen in 2019 when she rescued six kittens and their mom from under a trailer in Holland. When the kittens were three weeks old and starting to use a litter box, she noticed one of the babies wasn't pooping. Ivy was eventually diagnosed with *atresia ani with a rectovaginal fistula*—her rectal and anus area hadn't developed normally and the anus didn't open to eliminate stool. Ivy had a complete closure of her anus and an alternative route, referred to as a fistula, developed which exited through her vulva area. It took medicine, which gave Ivy diarrhea, and enemas to help her eliminate.

Nicole raised money for surgery to correct the issue. The first surgery, performed in Grand Rapids, didn't solve the problem. Nicole connected with a woman online who had a cat the with the same condition. She recommended a soft tissue specialist in Boston. Nicole and Ivy ended up traveling to Boston twice. Once for the surgery, and again for a revision—the opening had to be enlarged. Nicole and Ivy were on the last flight out of Boston before the airport was closed due to Covid-19.

Despite her rough beginning in life, Ivy is a loving cat and is doing well. "She's my pride and joy," Nicole said. Nicole also kept Ivy's brother, Mr. Pickles, who had a heart murmur and then congestive heart failure. He was taken to a specialist in Flint and is also doing fine.

Nicole's advocacy for cats will soon be expanding. She was stunned and humbled when her veterinarian, Dr. Angela Palen of the Laketown Cat Hospital in Saugatuck, recommended her when a gentleman client asked who might be interested in starting a cat sanctuary.

Nicole, who has met with the man, said he is willing to fund construction of a facility and help pay for its operating expenses. His only request is that the sanctuary be named after his cat, Scarlett.

Nicole said the paperwork is ready to submit for *Scarlett's Cat Sanctuary and Furry Friends Pet Recovery* to become a nonprofit. They have 15 acres in West Olive, just north of Zeeland, designated for the sanctuary.

Nicole wants to do it right so she's taking her time. She needs to figure out her boundaries and learn her limits. "I don't want to get in over my head, but I'm dedicated and determined," she said.

Her thoughts are to start small with a building used for intake and wellness center. Foster homes will be used when the cats and kittens are healthy.

Nicole's current mission is to reach out and meet people already involved in rescuing cats. She sees the big picture as a wagon wheel with every rescue being a spoke, and all of them meeting in the center to work together.

"Networking is huge, finding like-minded individuals and working together is important," she said.

I can't wait to see her plans come together.

Chapter 2

The Foot Soldiers of Cat Rescue

Some women prefer to be free agents, playing by their own rules but making a huge impact. They volunteer at rescues, do trap-neuter-return, open their homes to foster cats or care for neonatal orphan kittens. They socialize hissy, half-feral kittens, feed colonies of community cats or cruise social media for cats in desperate circumstances.

Such women come from all walks of life, but they have one thing in common: they love cats. Cats are their passion, sometimes their obsession.

While these women tend to work alone, they're all part of the rescue community. When they find a cat or kitten in need of help, they know who to call. In return, their phones ring and ping when one of their fellow cat advocates has a question or need.

It takes a village rings true in cat rescue.

In this chapter, you'll meet the foot soldiers of cat rescue. The women on the frontlines, getting their hands dirty and seeing the ugly result of the overpopulation of cats. Women who save countless lives and prevent countless more from being born into a world that, for the most part, still sees cats as disposable.

Cynthia Bailey and Turk.

Giving Community Cats a Home

Several years ago, a black cat befriended Cynthia Bailey. Little did she know the chance meeting would change her life and turn her into a crazy cat lady.

"She's the cat that got me into this mess," Cynthia admitted with a laugh as she told me the story of Midnight, while we sat in the backyard of her southeast Grand Rapids home.

Turned out Midnight was not only homeless, she was in the family way and chose Cynthia's front porch for her maternity ward—probably because the porch had been transformed into a "cat-utopia" for the expectant mother. A large dog kennel provided a cozy hide-a-way that any stray cat would gladly call home. The shelter, insulated and waterproofed, was concealed beneath a camouflage tent, the kind designed to hide hunters from their prey.

Despite the disguise, Cynthia's mail carrier noticed Midnight and her kittens and offered to get the family spayed/neutered.

That mail carrier was Gina Marvin, an advocate for stray cats. Gina founded Focus on Ferals after seeing so many homeless cats and kittens on her mail route. Gina taught Cynthia about TNR. Cynthia also learned a female cat can become pregnant as early as five months of age and have two to three litters per year.

"All I was doing back then was feeding," Cynthia recalled.

Since those lessons on cat reproduction and TNR, any cat who is a regular at Cynthia's back-porch feeding station earns itself an appointment at a spay/neuter clinic.

I first met Cynthia when I visited West Michigan Advanced Toastmasters. The club's meeting was in progress when a sobbing woman walked in, her entrance brought everything to a silent standstill. Then someone asked her what was wrong. She told the group she had just witnessed one of her cats being killed by dogs. I wondered if the woman was a member of the club or someone who lived nearby. Turned out she was a member. I remember thinking she was someone I needed to get to know, and I did. Our mutual interests of public speaking and cats made us instant friends. Cynthia loves telling stories, especially about her cats.

With enthusiasm she shared this tale: one day a coworker gave her a ride home. As they said their goodbyes, they noticed a gray cat strolling down the sidewalk. The cat stopped in front of each house and stared for a second.
"It was like he was reading the addresses," Cynthia joked.

When the traveler reached Cynthia's house, he

stopped, stared and then walked up her driveway to the backyard.

"Is that your cat?" the co-worker asked.

Cynthia shook her head no. She had never seen the cat before, but she wasn't surprised by another stray making its way to her feeding station. Cynthia claims she is well known on the *Cat-ernet*, the feline version of the Internet where cats share pertinent information such as where to get a free meal or warm bed.

The newcomer didn't remain a stranger. When he started following Cynthia everywhere she went, she named him Shadow.

When I interviewed Cynthia, she was taking care of five community cats, cats who weren't owned by anyone but were part of the community. She named each after a personality or appearance trait.

For instance, Smooth had a smooth gray coat and was known for being late to dinner.

Baker was the 13th cat she had neutered and was named after a baker's dozen.

Turq was a black cat with beautiful turquoise eyes.

Tweed had beautiful fur that looked like tweed cloth.

Whiskas was a tuxedo kitty whose white whiskers contrasted against black fur.

At one time, Cynthia had 11 cats in her colony. "Time takes its toll," she said with sadness. Recently one of her cats, Linus, had been hit and killed in the road.

"I was wailing. It hurt. I was distraught," she said softly, but added when she went to church that week the priest talked about a woman who had lost her baby when she was five months pregnant.

"That dried my tears," she said.

She's thankful she knows what happened to Linus. She's tormented by the cats who just disappear. "Not knowing bothers me more."

Cynthia's backyard has become a pet cemetery.

"Don't ask how many I have buried," she said. One of the cats buried is Midnight. She spotted him dead in a backyard tree. She knows he didn't die in the tree. Someone had to have flung his body up into the branches. Not everyone in the neighborhood appreciates cats.

Also buried is Tux, the cat mauled by neighbor dogs. He was the cat she was mourning when we first met. Large rocks mark the graves and it's common for cats to sit on the markers. Cynthia likes to think they're visiting their deceased buddies.

The cats in Cynthia's care get five-star treatment. Fresh food and water are served twice a day in a covered feeding station on her back porch.

A backyard tool shed has been converted into an apartment complex for the outsiders. An opening under an eave provides a hidden entrance. On a table inside the shed are two large Styrofoam containers. Each has a small hole for cats to access the straw-filled sleeping quarters.

Also, in the backyard was a cathouse Cynthia paid a guy to build—she found the blueprint for the dwelling online. The house is insulated and full of straw, making it a cozy nest on chilly days. The roof lifts up for cleaning.

Besides caring for the colony of cats in her yard, Cynthia socializes hissy, spit-fire kittens. Without human contact, the little ones would grow up to be feral. Socialization is most successful when kittens are younger than three months old.

At the time of our interview, she was working with three youngsters from Focus on Ferals.

"They're not at the lovey-dovey stage yet," she said of the kittens housed in a small bathroom.

She has socializing broken down into a step-by-step process. During the first couple of weeks she's just a housekeeper, cleaning and feeding. "I don't even try to touch them," she said, adding that the kittens usually hide from her.

Cynthia feeds the kittens, as well as her outside cats, in muffin tins so each cat has its own compartment of food. Cynthia said she wouldn't care to eat from a communal food dish so she doesn't think cats do either. She also warms the canned food. She doesn't like cold food so she assumes cats won't either.

After a couple weeks of just feeding and cleaning, Cynthia said kittens get curious and start coming out of hiding when she is doing the chores. She then brings in passive toys like fake mice and small balls. Next, she offers interactive toys such as dangly things on a string.

Then she starts to touch the kittens, giving them back and belly rubs. Before long the little ones beg for attention and are eager to sit on her lap. At that point it's time to say good-bye as the kittens are ready for their forever homes.

Cynthia has always been an animal person. When she was young, she wanted to be a veterinarian, but now knows she sold herself short by not believing she was smart enough. Instead, she became an x-ray technician and has worked in trauma hospitals in Chicago and the Bay Area of California.

When her mother died, Cynthia inherited her house in Grand Rapids and decided to leave the West Coast. Since moving to Michigan, she has worked a variety of jobs. Now a widow of retirement age, Cynthia prefers to keep working. She recently returned to college—just because she loves learning. It's also why she's a member of Toastmasters.

Another one of her favorite cat stories happened on Halloween when Midnight was still alive. Cynthia decorated her porch for the holiday: a plastic wrap, sporting a witch riding a broom against a full moon, covered the front door. A caldron, filled with hot water, gave off a mist in the cool evening air. A gigantic spider web stretched over the porch complete with entangled bugs. There was a big bowl of candy.

Cynthia dressed as a witch in a black dress and pointy hat. Her Halloween voice cackled like that of a wicked woman with demonic powers.

"I'm all in for Halloween, but I don't get many trick-or-treaters," she said. Sometimes she'd step down from the porch to drum up business for her candy giveaway. Neighborhood kids who knew her weren't scared, but anyone who just happened to be passing by would do a double take and usually scurry away. She recalled the time she spotted a man approaching and decided to wait for him in the shadows.

"Excuse me, sir," she cackled in her best witch's voice. "Would you like some candy?"

She said he hesitated for a moment but then reached into the bowl. That's when Midnight made her debut, running full speed directly between them.

"A black cat?" he said in a panic.

"Pay no attention to that cat—it used to be a little boy."

Apparently, the black cat was too much and the stranger took off running at full speed.

"Come back," she yelled. "It's Halloween."

He didn't stop.

"He's probably still running," Cynthia said with delight.

Melody Cassady with a cat at Faithful to Felines.

From Key Largo to Muskegon; Doing What's Needed

Melody Cassady's phone continually dinged with text alerts as we talked. A farmer needed help with barn cats, could she assess the situation? There's an injured cat, could she pick it up? Cats needed to be transported, was she available? A cat needed a foster home, did she have room? Kittens needed to be socialized, did she have time? A feral cat gave birth to five kittens in a garbage can, was there anyone who could help?

For five years, Mel was an animal control officer in Key Largo, Florida, but then she met a man online from Muskegon and decided to give our northern state a try. She visited Michigan several times before making the move in 2006 with five cats and a dog.

The guy was a good fit until he retired. He wanted to spend the next chapter of his life sailing in the Bahamas. Mel had already devoted 15 years of her life to sailing, and she didn't want to return to that lifestyle. So, he left to follow his dream and she stayed to follow her passion for working with animals.

One of the cats who made the move to Michigan with Mel was her sailing partner. She picked up the tuxedo kitty on a dock in Venezuela. She named him Hurricane because the year he was born, 1995, was a bad year for hurricanes.

"He always did night watch with me," she recalled. Hurricane wore a harness to keep him safe during night duty.

The first time I saw Melody, she was walking a dog outside Petco in Muskegon. I was there to interview people who were working an adoption event, so I stopped and chatted with her. At the time, she was volunteering for Pound Buddies Rescue. After meeting her, it seemed whatever pet-related event I went to, Mel would be there. Throughout the years, she has volunteered or worked for several animal-related organizations in the Muskegon area.

For the past few years, Mel has devoted her time to cats. "The biggest need is with cats," she explained.

Mel has live-trapped hundreds of cats starting in Key Largo where it took her two years to TNR all the cats in one of the trailer parks. In Muskegon County, Mel said it's common for people to feed neighborhood cats but few accept the responsibility to spay/neuter.

Theoretically, a cat can give birth to three litters of kittens per year, with an average of four kittens per litter. If the cat lives 15 years this could result in up to 180 kittens. If half of those kittens are females, it's easy to see why there are so many cats.

Mel has done a lot of trapping in mobile home parks in Muskegon County. She said she cleaned up Bel Air Estates six years ago, but it's full of cats again. Mobile home parks attract low-income people who acquire pets and don't have the resources to take care of them. Cats are also frequently left behind when people move.

One of Mel's recent projects was a farm in Ravenna. She trapped ten kittens who were fixed, socialized and placed for adoption. She also trapped six adult cats, got them fixed and returned them to the barn.

In a neighborhood in Muskegon Heights, she had already trapped 18 adult cats. She also caught and removed 14 kittens from the same area. That TNR project was still active when we talked.

Mel recalls a report she once read that stated the mortality rate of feral kittens was 50 to 75 percent. Survival depended on the mother's access to food and shelter. Feral kittens can starve to death, or fall victim to upper respiratory infections, wormy bellies and flea infestations. If they are born when it's cold, hypothermia can take their lives. Raccoons and other predators also kill kittens.

Thinking of the fate of those kittens is a driving force behind Mel's ambition.

Mel volunteers for any group that requests help including Heaven Can Wait, Faithful to Felines and Muskegon Humane Society. She fosters cats, does TNR, helps with adoptions and performs euthanasia. Mel was certified in euthanasia when she was an animal control officer and offers her services to rescues when cats are beyond help.

"Whatever needs to be done," she said.

For a while, Mel worked at the West Michigan Spay & Neuter Clinic in Fruitport, but quit because the regular hours interfered with her mission to help cats.

"TNR is time consuming," she said.

Traps have to be set and monitored. If a cat is caught, the trap has to be covered to calm the animal and taken to a safe place until it can be transported to a clinic. The day following surgery, the cat has to be picked up. If possible, the cat is kept in a quiet place to allow healing before it's returned to where it was caught.

Mel is thankful for low-cost spay/neuter clinics, such as West Michigan Spay & Neuter and C-SNIP in Grand Rapids. She's also thankful for the Bissell Pet Foundation and the Petco Foundation for the grants they give to the clinics and rescues to help with expenses.

Mel said more and more people, even farmers, are getting their pets fixed, but she's still not optimistic about the future.

"I don't know if we'll ever solve the cat problem," she said. But that won't stop her from spending her retirement years trying. "It's what I do. There's satisfaction in helping."

Mel doesn't consider herself a crazy cat lady. Instead, she thinks of herself as a crazy animal person. Instead of squishing spiders who take up residency in her home, she catches the multi-legged critters and releases them outside. She is a vegan, meaning she doesn't eat meat or any animal byproducts such as eggs and dairy.

Her path to becoming a vegan began when she was on a medication for migraines that caused her to lose her taste for red meat. She started eating more chicken, but then read an article about cancerous flesh being cut off slaughtered chickens and the meat still sold for human consumption. So, she eliminated chicken from her diet and started eating more fish. Then she learned how to scuba dive and enjoyed swimming among fish; subsequently, she quit eating fish. A book on factory farms convinced her to give up eggs and dairy.

"It's so sad, the way we treat animals," she said.

George Johnson and Sandi DeHaan with
George's cat Gimpy.

Southside Sandi

For several years, Sandi DeHaan volunteered for the Humane Society of West Michigan. She walked dogs, took cats and dogs to a local television station on Fridays to have them highlighted for adoption, and she worked in the cat isolation room cleaning cages.

Helping at the humane society made Sandi aware of the plight of homeless cats in West Michigan.

As a nurse, Sandi worked in in-home health care. When a client, who lived in a manufactured home park, had a cat with five kittens living under her trailer, Sandi borrowed a live trap and caught the mom cat and kittens. She socialized the kittens and took them to Dr. Jen at Crash's Landing—this was years ago when Dr. Jen still took in kittens. Sandi soon left the humane society and started volunteering at Crash's. That was 19 years ago.

In 2013, when visiting a client in Grand Rapids, Sandi noticed several cats lounging on the porch of a neighboring house. She knocked on the door, talked to the homeowner, and offered to get the cats spayed/neutered, but her offer was declined. The next spring, when several kittens were added to the porch-dwellers, the home-owner asked her for help.

Sandi started to watch for cats when she visited clients. At Walden Woods, a senior apartment complex in Wyoming, she met two elderly people who were feeding outside strays. Sandi offered to help and, working together, they live-trapped the cats, got them fixed and returned them to where they were caught.

When necessary, Sandi supplies the outside cats with shelters—either an 18-gallon plastic storage container lined with Styrofoam and filled with straw or a plain Styrofoam cooler filled with straw.

If the cats she traps don't have a caretaker, Sandi feels a sense of responsibility towards them. "Once you trap them, you have to feed them," she said.

Through TNR, Sandi met Cheryl Gachter, a like-minded woman, who also had a mission of taking care of homeless cats.

Every day, either Sandi or Cheryl make the rounds to 17 feeding stations throughout the south side of Grand Rapids to supply fresh water and food to cat colonies. On Sundays, Sandi has extra stops. A mail carrier, nicknamed Flash, feeds community cats as she delivers mail. Sandi fills in for Flash on her day off and when she takes vacation.

I rode along with Sandi on a cold January day. Someone had told me about an amazing woman who was devoted to helping community cats. I called her and she invited me to join her on her daily rounds.

The first order of business was to load her car with supplies—paper towels for cleaning bowls, canned food, dry food and jugs of fresh water. Sandi also carried a shovel for snow removal from around cat shelters.

The feeding stations were in garages, backyards, vacant lots, behind guard rails and on porches. Sandi cleaned the bowls, filled one with fresh water, and others with dry kibble topped with scoops of canned food. Sandi feeds high-quality food, which the cats need to survive outside. It took about three hours to complete the route.

Some cats were friendly—obviously once pets but for unknown reasons now live on the streets. Such was the case of Lionel, the women name the cats in their care. Lionel, a big gray and white boy, not only wanted food, he wanted attention. He rubbed on Sandi's legs, making it difficult for her to walk. Lionel lived with Shelby and Caboose in a wooded area at the end of a dead-end street. The location, near train tracks, inspired the train-related names. The area was littered with trash—apparently a dumping ground for more than just cats.

When Sandi finds kittens or friendly adults, she has a list of friends and rescues she calls on for help. Can someone provide a foster home? Or take them into their adoption program?

"I'm grateful for the network of helpers and resources I have," she said. Sometimes the cat is placed on a waiting list at Crash's or the humane society.

Sandi thought Lionel was a candidate for adoption and eventually got him into Crash's Landing, where he was fostered and then adopted by a volunteer.

"He's doing great. I get to visit him," Sandi said. "If I can get a cat off the street, that's the frosting on the cake."

It was Dr. Jen, founder of Crash's Landing, who nicknamed her Southside Sandi.

"Dr. Jen is my lifeline," Sandi said.

Sandi worries about breaking up friendships when she rescues a friendly cat. Such was the case of Curline and Violet. The two kitties shared a shelter and had been best buddies for seven years. When Curline quit eating, Sandi took her to Dr. Jen. Curline's teeth were rotten and had to be pulled. Dr. Jen also suspected a spot on Curline's head was cancerous, and recommended not putting the aging sick kitty back outside.

Curline was resting comfortably in a cage in Sandi's living room when I visited.

"I don't know what to do," Sandi said. Should she try to find Curline an inside home? If she did, Violet would be alone. Violet was weary of people and probably wouldn't appreciate being caught and brought inside. The decision was made when the cancer diagnosis was confirmed. Curline remained an inside cat until she was euthanized, and Violet was left outside.

Another cat now eats with Violet when Sandi serves dinner, but Violet doesn't share her shelter with anyone.

As we made the rounds that wintery day, most cats recognized Sandi's car and left the warmth of their beds to greet her. Some watched from a distance, anticipating their daily meal.

"I'm as happy to see them as they are to see me," Sandi said. One of the heartbreaking aspects of caring for community cats is sometimes they disappear.

Sandi frequently gets calls from people, some she doesn't even know, asking for help. She does her best to help even if it means paying for surgeries and food out of her own pocket. Sometimes she brings the cats to her home until she can arrange for them to go elsewhere.

"There are times I can't take one more cat in my house," she said. "Cat rescue is like a full-time job, and my house is like a humane society."

A friend of Sandi's set up up a GoFundMe campaign that raised $600. But it didn't take long to spend the money when feeding dozens of cats and paying veterinarian costs. People she helps sometimes donate, but often Sandi pays for expenses herself.

Sandi eventually retired from her job, but retirement didn't last long. "I needed money for cat rescue," she said, explaining why she continued to work part-time doing in-home health care.

While Sandi hasn't had a vacation in years, and taking care of the cats is financially and emotional draining, she isn't about to quit. "I don't know how I can stop. I can't just stop feeding them," she said.

In 2021, Sandi's husband died. She quit her part-time job and readied their northern Michigan cottage to sell. Sandi's only son had died years before.

Being alone, Sandi realized how thankful she was to be involved in cat rescue. "Everybody has to have a purpose in their life. This is my purpose," she said.

Last year, a woman she helped with TNR told her of a man she should meet who rescued cats not far from where Sandi lived. Sandi told her to give the guy her number and have him call.

When the man called, he introduced himself as George Johnson and said he once put together a family tree and the name DeHaan was in it. Sandi had kept her maiden name when she married, and she recalled hearing about a distant relative who worked on a family tree.

"I always wanted to meet him," Sandi said. But she didn't know the man's name or where he lived. She didn't even know which state he resided in.

After a discussion about relatives, George and Sandi realized they were related. Sandi's paternal grandfather's sister was George's mother.

George, who is 81 years old, now rides with Sandi when she makes her rounds caring for the colonies of cats. "It's nice to have someone go with me," she said. George picks up trash while she does the feeding. He's learned the names of all the cats.

When I recently talked with Sandi, she said she's as busy as ever. She's been getting calls from people being evicted who are feeding outside cats and don't know what to do. She also gets calls from people who are moving and can't take their cats. She knows if she doesn't get involved the cats will be left outside or dumped somewhere.

146

"I have to advocate for cats. It's where my heart is. I wish I could do more," she said.

Kim Grant and Thomas.

Food for the Soul

If you peek into Kim Grant's car, you'll see a rescue kit that includes a cat carrier, towels, a leash, and food and treats for both cats and dogs.

She used the kit a few days before our interview. After leaving an exercise class, she noticed a cat hanging out in the bushes. She caught the dilute tortie and looked for an owner, but couldn't find one, so she took the kitty home. She posted a photo of the kitty on Facebook and asked her friends for name suggestions. The one that stuck was London Fog.

Kim took the cat to C-SNIP, a local low-cost spay/neuter clinic, and had her spayed. She debated with herself on what to do with London Fog. Find her a home or return her to where she was found? She opted to return London Fog to the inner-city neighborhood where she had been picked up. Later Kim regretted the decision. She returned to look for the tortie and instead found a friendly calico. This one won the name Meg White.

Kim got Meg White fixed and was able to get her on a waiting list for admission to the adoption program at a nearby rescue. She continued to look for London Fog.

For Kim it's a no-brainer to get involved. "You see a need and you act on it," she said.

In 2015, Kim's friend, Emily Stalsonburg, saw a plea for help on Facebook about a cat stranded in a tree on Fair Street in a residential/industrial area in southeast Grand Rapids. With the help of a tree-climbing friend, Emily and her husband were able to get the cat down. Emily invited Kim to go with her to ask the cat owner to relinquish ownership so their veterinarian could treat the rescued cat. While there, they were approached by a kid who asked, "Do you want to see the nine kittens up the block?"

Sure enough, a mom-cat with nine kittens romped in the yard of one of the houses. The homeowner didn't want the kittens, but he didn't want them taken to the animal shelter where he thought they would be euthanized. He accepted their offer to get the cat family fixed and to find them homes.

"We proceeded like fools to catch the cats," Kim said.

That was the beginning of the Fair Street Project. Over the next 18 months, Emily and Kim trapped 54 cats and kittens in the neighborhood. They found homes for 51. Only three were unadoptable and returned to where they had been caught.

"I like catching a cat and changing the course of its life. It feeds my soul," Kim said.

Kim has nine cats, three of them came from Fair

Street. "Crazy is double digits," she joked. In the calculation, she didn't include the ferals who hangout in her yard, depend on her for food and find refuge in the shelters she provides.

When she was young, Kim's parents limited her to one cat. "When I got my own home, they multiplied quickly," she laughed. The first cat she adopted was Gus. She called him her soulmate, recognizing it was a weird word to use for a cat but the only word she could find that fit their relationship.

"I love them all ridiculously, but Gus was the bee's knees. He was my whole heart," she said. Gus was adopted from the Humane Society of West Michigan and suffered from inflammatory bowel disease (IBD). "There's not a disease I hate more." Gus succumbed to IBD after six years of fighting the disorder.

For three years, Kim volunteered at the humane society as a member of the Wednesday Night Crew who worked in the cattery. She noticed the photos used on the Internet of cats available for adoption looked like mug shots. Since photos play a significant role in attracting adopters, she offered to photograph the cats. She created a photo booth and, with the help of a friend who entertained the cats with toys, took photos that portrayed the individuality of each animal.

Kim quit volunteering at the humane society when a cat she tried to adopt was euthanized for "loose stool". She felt the condition could have been easily treated and didn't think it justified a death sentence.

"It left a bad taste," she said.

Kim then started volunteering for Crash's Landing, a cat rescue in Grand Rapids that specialized in helping stray cats. She volunteered there for ten years.

I first became aware of Kim while she volunteered at Crash's. As a graphic designer, she used to create Crash's ads for *Cats and Dogs Magazine*. We became friends on Facebook, and that's how I learned just how crazy she was about cats.

Kim makes sure the community cats in her Alger Heights neighborhood are taken care of and aren't reproducing. On a warm September evening a few years ago, she saw a cat staring at her through the kitchen window. The next day, she took the super friendly kitty to her veterinarian and had it scanned for a microchip. She was elated when one was found. But when the owners were called, she learned that they had moved and didn't want the cat anymore, and had left it behind.

"She was so sassy and beautiful," Kim said. The cat, now named Jackie, had a checkup and received vaccines. A few days later, she quit eating. Blood work revealed she had immune-mediated anemia. Her condition was stabilized with steroids, but whenever they tried to wean her off the drugs, she became anemic.

"She wasn't a good candidate for adoption, and I love a hot mess," Kim said. So, Jackie became a part of her feline family.

Kim now volunteers for several area cat rescues. "It feels good to be a cog in the wheel of change," she said.

Kim has become an expert on caring for sick, neonatal kittens. She shares their stories on social media and has a following of like-minded feline lovers who support her work though prayers, healing energy and donations.

In May 2020, Sandi DeHaan brought Kim two tiny kittens, only hours old. "Those two were definitely the smallest neonates I have ever worked with," she said.

Greyson was a sleek, short-haired, solid gray boy and Blaze was a beautiful medium-haired tortie. Blaze was born with a prolapsed anus that would need corrective surgery when she was old enough. Aside from that, they were healthy and easily met each weekly milestone.

When the kittens were about five weeks old, they outgrew Kim's bathroom, which was the only place she had available for them. At the time her work schedule was unpredictable, so she asked her mom if she would foster the kittens until Blaze was old enough for surgery.

"My dad had passed away in February and my mom's cat, Roxie, had passed in April. I thought having these two kittens would be a good distraction and help ease the pain of such a sad time," Kim explained.

Around three weeks into her fostering, Kim received a text from her mom that Blaze's behind looked normal, literally overnight. The issue had resolved itself. That meant the kittens were ready to be fixed, vaccinated and placed for adoption. The day the kittens went for their spay/neuter surgeries, Kim's mom said that the house was too quiet without them, and she wanted to adopt the pair.

"They have grown into stunning cats and fill her days

153

with laugh-out-loud silly antics, lots of cuddles and love," Kim said.

To help pay the expenses of the kittens and cats in her care, Kim makes cat toys and sells them online at www.kgrantdesigns.etsy.com. All the toys are handmade. She started out making them as gifts for friends, then as fundraisers for Crash's, then Etsy came along and she jumped on board. Thirteen years and more than 7,000 sales later, she's still making cats happy all over the world, literally.

By day, Kim is a packaging designer. She brings that same attention to detail to the packaging for her catnip toys—fortune cookies come in a to-go box, strawberries come in a real berry basket and olives come in a martini glass.

"I like to think that the toys delight the cats and the packaging delights the people," she said.

Kim's love for cats has impacted her entire life. She is dumbfounded by the cruelty to animals she sees every day. From pets that are considered disposable, to the food people eat, to leather—the skin of animals.

Because of that cruelty, Kim has become a vegan. She doesn't eat meat, eggs, nor dairy products. She doesn't wear leather and purchases only cruelty-free products that haven't been tested on animals or don't contain ingredients derived from animals.

"It's hard to be compassionate to one species and not the others; be kind to every kind," she said.

If you're interested in Kim's catnip toys, visit www.kgrantdesigns.etsy.com.

Savannah Matarazzo with Hodor.

The Cherry Valley Project

The adage "be careful what you wish for" rings true for Savannah Matarazzo. One day after the 22-year-old Caledonia woman wished for a TNR project close to her home, she learned about a farm with an overpopulation problem offering free barn cats only two miles from where she lived.

"I was thinking of a project with maybe ten cats," said Savannah, who volunteered for Carol's Ferals, a group that specialized in TNR.

It was January 2018 when Savannah and her husband, Seth, investigated the free-cat offer. From the road, the homestead looked picturesque—a white farmhouse, several outbuildings including red wooden barns, and red and teal pole barns. There was minimum outside clutter. The owners, a couple in their 90s, had lived there since 1942. At some point they quit farming and started leasing their land to other farmers, leaving the barns unused except for storage.

Savannah said the couple's children knew their parents were feeding barn cats, but they had no idea how many. That is, until medical issues intervened. Mom broke her leg. Dad developed a heart condition. And the truth came out—the couple was spending more than $150 per week feeding what they thought were around 60 cats.

The attractiveness of the homestead was superficial. While the outside of the barns looked clean and well maintained, their insides were a stark contrast. They were filthy and crammed full of stuff—farm equipment, tires, old furniture, tools, boats, campers, boxes of newspapers, clothes, dozens of empty cat food bags, trash and so much more. Savannah guessed in all the years the family lived there they had never thrown anything away. They just stored it in one of the outbuildings.

"The conditions were disgusting," she said.

Then there were the cats: adult cats, kittens, pregnant cats, injured cats, sick cats and dead cats.

Savannah said she had to get involved after seeing the cats and the conditions they lived in. The filth, the noxious odor, the freezing cold—cats were actually freezing to death. She found two cats impaled on the tines of a hay rake. Even though the cats were free to leave, they were dependent on the food provided by the property owners.

"I drive by that place several times a day. I couldn't continue to drive past it knowing those cats were there," she said.

Savannah and Carol Manos, the founder of Carol's Ferals, discussed the options. They knew if animal control was called, the cats would be trapped and euthanized due to the high number of cats and because the majority of them were feral. Savannah wanted to give the animals a chance and offered to do the trapping. The family accepted the help, but they wanted the cats removed—not returned. They only wanted to have a couple barn cats.

I saw a post on Carol's Ferals' Facebook page about a TNR project at a farm with more than 100 cats. It sounded like a story for *Cats and Dogs Magazine,* so I sent a message and asked who I could interview. Savannah answered and was willing to talk to me. When we met, it was an *ah-ha* moment for both of us. She told me she had been reading my magazine since she was a little kid, and it helped inspire her to get involved in rescue. She was thrilled to be interviewed. She called it a full-circle moment—from reading the magazine to being featured in it. Her reaction made me realize I had been publishing the magazine a long time—close to 12 years. It also made me aware that I would never know the full extent of the impact *Cats and Dogs Magazine* had on the people who read it.

Savannah took me on a tour of the farm. The conditions were as horrendous as she described. Kudos to her for taking on the task of trapping the cats.

"There's been a few times I bawled while being there; I just wanted to leave," she said. "I didn't want to find any more dead, dying or injured cats. But I couldn't make myself leave. I knew the rest (of the cats) would end up the same way, and I couldn't do that to them."

As the cats were live-trapped, they were taken to

Carol's Ferals where they were evaluated and received medical treatment. A room at Carol's facility was set aside for the project and became known as the Cherry Valley Cats Room—named after the location of the farm.

About 90 percent of the cats had upper respiratory infections and roundworm infestations. They were also under weight, malnourished and dehydrated. Some had chronic diarrhea, leading to skin burns and infections.

Two cats had wounds suspected to be coyote bites. When a dead coyote was spotted in the road near the farm, it confirmed the suspicion.

The medical expense was overwhelming. The owners of the farm agreed to pay $50 per cat to have them removed, but that didn't come close to covering the cost of providing medical care, spay/neuter surgeries, vaccines, food and litter. Fundraisers were started and caring community members donated to help with expenses.

Friendly cats were put into Carol's adoption program. If the cats were feral and needed to be outside, they were housed temporarily in barns owned by volunteers.

At the farm, a litter of eight kittens was discovered along with a single kitten from a different litter. Savannah said eight kittens is a huge litter for a healthy mom-cat. For a malnourished cat, estimated to be only six months old herself and living under stressful conditions, the situation wasn't good. Savannah, who has a passion for taking care of kittens, took the babies home, but despite her best care, four died, as did the solo kitten due to pneumonia

One of the kittens Savannah bottle-fed didn't keep up with his littermates, so she took him to a veterinarian who diagnosed the kitten with hydrocephalus. Hydrocephalus, which literally means "water on the brain," is a buildup of fluid inside the skull. The accumulation puts pressure on the brain and can cause such things as an enlarged, dome-shaped head, seizures, blindness and behavioral changes. Symptoms vary depending on the severity of the condition.

The vet suggested euthanasia, that the kitten was "not worth" trying to save. Savannah refused to have the kitten euthanized and got a second opinion. The second vet said the kitten, who Savannah named Hodor, might not make it but there was a treatment that could be tried.

Savannah officially adopted Hodor. His coordination isn't the best—he walks and falls like a drunk, but he continually improves. She also kept his brother and two other kittens with medical issues.

By the end of April, Savannah had trapped 88 cats. She guessed there were about a dozen more to catch. But trapping had to be put on hold because the Cherry Valley Cats Room was full. Savannah explained that trapping was easy, but since the cats weren't being returned to the farm, it took time to find new homes for them, and they all required care while waiting.

Six months after she started, Savannah removed the last two cats and several week-old kittens from the property. The total number of cats trapped was 108, but two cats who had been trapped gave birth at Carol's, bringing the grand total for the project to 115. Only 13 cats, including seven kittens, didn't survive. One cat, who had an eye torn from its socket and an infected face, had to be euthanized. The others had various medical problems.

It took one year, eight months and 21 days from the day Savannah started trapping, for the last feral cat to be taken to a new home in a barn.

It took three years, two months and one day from the day Savannah started trapping, for the last friendly cat to be adopted.

"I'm not sure how I did it," Savannah said four years after starting the Cherry Valley Project. She credits her husband with being understanding, or tolerant at the very least, and said he liked playing with the kittens. "Big tough men are only tough until you show them a kitten," she joked.

At the time, the young couple was living with Savannah's parents, and Savannah is very thankful her folks allowed her to bring cats and kittens into their home. "My mom helped with the care of the cats kept at our house, from cleaning to helping with medications to helping socialize the timid cats. My parents put up with a lot in their house for a while."

Trapping, taking care of the cats at Carol's Ferals, and bottle feeding the kittens became so time consuming, Savannah had to cut her hours as a home health care aide. Before becoming a home health care aide, Savannah had been in the Air National Guard, but she was discharged for medical reasons. She has asthma, degenerative disc disorder, and narcolepsy. In the Guard she was a Black Hawk mechanic and was training to be a crew chief.

For a time, she worked at Carol's Ferals as an assistant care technician. Today Savannah works full time at a veterinarian clinic as a technician assistant. When she has time, she'd like to get back into TNR. She hopes to go to college and study veterinarian medicine with a major in genetics and virology.

While Savannah admits she wasn't always a cat person, the Cherry Valley Project changed her. "I've morphed into a cat lady. Now cats are my thing. They're interesting creatures with personality and attitude. Each one is their own individual."

Lynnette Wieck (left) and Maureen Herendeen.

Helping Street Cats

They describe themselves as two old retired ladies. It's true Maureen Herendeen and Lynnette Wieck no longer receive paychecks, but they're definitely still working. As for old, age is just a number. What counts is energy and passion, and these two women have both.

Lynnette and Maureen are advocates for street cats. Their passion is TNR of community cats in Kent County, especially in Grand Rapids. The women first met at Carol's Ferals. They reconnected at a hoarder's house. "We spent a ton of time trapping and talked while we waited," Maureen recalled. When trying to catch an outside cat, the trap is set and the trappers back off and wait and wait and wait, hoping the cat will take the bait.

At the time, Lynnette was trying to ease out of cat rescue and move into retirement after spending 39 years working in Meijer's corporate offices.

Maureen had recently retired from nursing and had founded Feral Cat Solutions. The group received its

501(c)(3) nonprofit status shortly before our interview. We met at corporate headquarters—Maureen's home. Her living room doubled as the board room.

"I don't want the overhead of a building. I want to provide free services and get the friendlies off the streets," Maureen said.

Maureen had been volunteering for Carol's Ferals, but when Carol's closed she continued doing TNR on her own. She approached Kent County Animal Shelter (KCAS) and asked if they could help with the spay/neuter surgeries of cats she trapped.

"I couldn't ask for more cooperation from them," she said. Since the shelter had a staff veterinarian and a grant to cover surgery costs, they were able to give Maureen surgical appointments each week.

When Maureen and Lynnette reconnected, they discovered their personalities complemented each other, and they decided to join forces.

Maureen is an action person. "I move at warped speed," she said. "I do all the interacting with trappers, planning, collecting the cats, caring for the cats and transporting."

Lynnette is laid-back, detail oriented and spends a ton of time doing behind-the-scenes work. She also feeds feral cat colonies several days a week.

Lynnette is so organized that she can find the description of every single cat they have helped, where it came from and the client's name. The women plan to start mapping out where the cats come from on a large county map so they have a visual tool. They'll be able to see which neighborhoods have the most outdoor cats, the locations of colonies and the problem areas.

Maureen's goals with Feral Cat Solutions is to educate the public about TNR and to assist with feral cat management for homeowners and property managers plagued with abandoned cats.

Maureen and Lynnette have years of experience in cat rescue. They've both volunteered for various rescue groups and estimate each has already trapped hundreds of cats.

Lynnette volunteered at the Humane Society of West Michigan for 17 years. She was first introduced to TNR through Focus on Ferals when she discovered a need at a local farm overrun with cats and kittens.

Maureen got her start trapping cats when she lived in San Diego, California.

As word gets out about Feral Cat Solutions, Maureen is doing less trapping and more advising. She now loans live traps to people with outside cats that need to be fixed.

Unfortunately, there are some folks who don't want to do the work involved with TNR. Maureen said she's heard many excuses of why people can't trap.

"People can be so disrespectful. They don't understand we do this for free," she explained.

Lynnette agreed. "It's not fun. It's a need. It's our choice to help animals."

They will help trap for the elderly and disabled.

"People have to want to do it, to extend themselves, to

care," Maureen said. She was impressed when an 83-year-old woman borrowed traps and was able to catch the cats on her property.

Trapping is scheduled for five days each week. When the cats are caught, they're taken to Maureen's home in northeast Grand Rapid and she transports them to surgery. She has ten cages in her garage where cats stay before and after surgery.

"It's an elaborate dance of a schedule," Maureen said.

Not all the trapped cats are returned to the streets. "We give them a chance if they show any sign of being friendly," Lynnette said. When that happens, Maureen puts the cat in her Socialization Boot Camp, which means she lets the cats loose in her house and gives them time to become friendly.

"It can take a long time, but it's so rewarding. I feel like I won the lottery when they let me pet them," she said. She had seven in the program when we talked and at least 40 had already graduated from boot camp and were adopted.

Since starting Feral Cat Solutions in 2021, 711 cats have been trapped and spayed/neutered as of June 2022. More than 100 friendly cats have been trapped and placed into adoption programs at Second Chance Cats, Crash's Landing, Kent County Animal Shelter and the Humane Society of West Michigan. The ladies used to pay the intake fee out of their own pockets for the friendly cats to get into the adoption programs. Since they're both on fixed incomes, they have started to do fundraising on social media to help with expenses.

As the relationship with KCAS grows, Feral Cat Solutions receives more and more referrals from the county. One call regarded a family of three who had died of Covid-19 and left behind more than two dozen cats. Animal control had already taken 26 cats from inside the house. Maureen were asked to deal with the outside cats—a caretaker was found for the ferals and, if needed, the cats would be relocated.

Another call was about a 92-year-old woman who was in hospice and asked for help with outside cats. The women trapped 12. Two went to Maureen's Boot Camp and ten had to be relocated.

Maureen is proud of the relationship she has with KCAS. She urges cat lovers in other counties to do the same with their county shelter. She was told the shelter is feeling an impact from the work the women are doing. She hopes it's true, that less cats are being brought in, which means fewer cats are being euthanized.

"My biggest goal is to not be needed," Maureen said.

For more information, follow Feral Cat Solutions on Facebook or email feralcatsolutions2021@gmail.com.

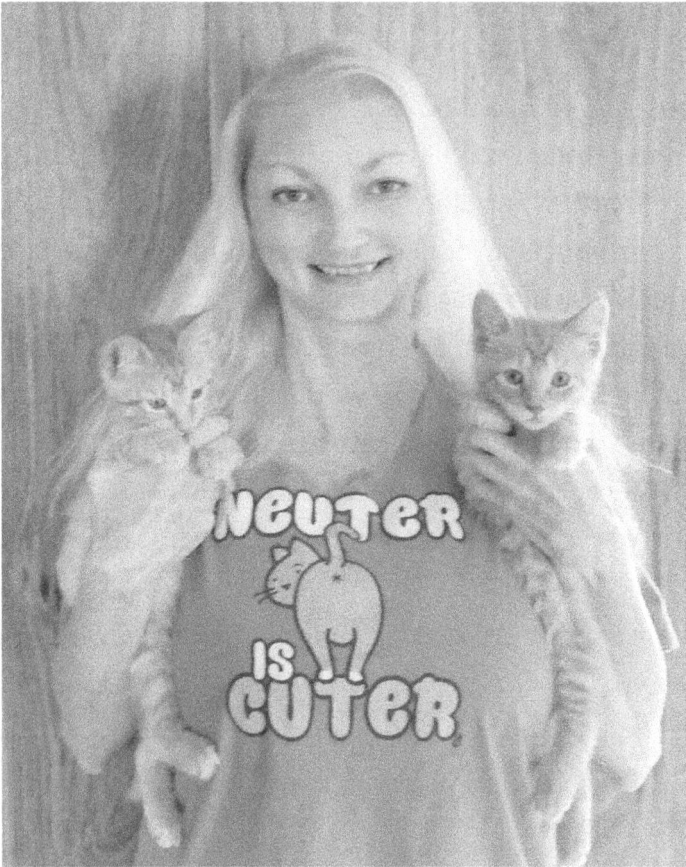

Tara Batema with fosters Gabe and George
from the Golden Globes litter.

Birth to Adoption

As far back as she can remember, Tara Batema has had a thing for pregnant cats. Maybe it's because when Tara was young, her Mom rescued a cat who later gave birth to four kittens.

"I was only 12 years old, loved cats, and had never experienced the birth of kittens before, probably not any birth. I was super excited for the kittens," she said. Two of Floofee's babies died, but the family kept the two survivors.

At a time when most cat rescues terminate the pregnancies of cats through spay surgeries, Tara's specializes in fostering pregnant cats. "I love raising kittens from birth to adoption," she said.

She realizes there is an overpopulation of cats, but doesn't see abort/spay as the answer, unless it's an early-stage pregnancy.

"If I can see they're pregnant, I wouldn't do it," Tara said.

Tara has Ehlers-Danlos Syndrome (EDS), a rare genetic connective-tissue disorder that causes a shortened life expectancy—her Dad passed from EDS when he was 41. Tara is now 44.

"I was born with it. It's my normal. I've learned my limitations and I find happiness in little things," she said. One of those things is kittens.

When Tara was 26 years old, she was hospitalized with her first life-threatening rupture caused from the disorder. As she lay in her hospital bed wondering if she was going to die, she recalled her childhood cat Floofee, and realized one of her regrets was not having raised another litter of kittens.

Upon learning how her daughter felt, Tara's Mom bought her a purebred Somali named Veeshan. At one-point, Tara thought she would become a breeder and bought a second Somali named Freya. She did breed Freya and the result was five kittens.

"I never sold any of them," she said. Two went to a cousin and Tara kept three. She called them her A Team, all the kittens' names started with the letter A. She never bred her cats again. Instead her life took a different direction.

"It started with a pair of shoes," Tara said. Chunky, flowered, platform shoes that people called "pinup shoes." Pinups, images of sexy women designed to be pinned up on a wall, were originally used in advertisements and became popular during World War II.

The comments about her shoes led Tara to enter a

pinup contest at the Metro Cruise in Grand Rapids. She didn't win. She didn't even place. But she did get involved with a pinup charity group that helped veterans.

Then one day at her Mom's house in Hamilton, Tara thought she saw a squirrel in the driveway. Her eyes were deceiving her; it wasn't a squirrel, it was a starving, dehydrated gray kitten.

"I couldn't afford to keep it, but I did anyways," she said. She named the kitten Hope and she became the ambassador for Tara's Facebook page; a Touch of Cats.

Online, Tara started following Tiny Kittens, The Kitten Lady and Kitten Academy.

I want to do this she remembers thinking.

She became a Facebook friend with Chalsey Schmidt who volunteered for Piper's Palace, a cat rescue in nearby Zeeland. Chalsey later started her own rescue, Kittens in the Mitten. Through Chalsey, Tara started to foster kittens. Her first litter was four kittens found under a porch in Flint. They were named the Flintstones.

"They were feral," Tara said. She put them in a spare bedroom and then couldn't catch them. She learned a big lesson. "You don't know what you're going to get until you get them, and it's always harder than you think it's going to be," she said. "You have to love cats."

The Flintstones were eventually tamed, spayed/neutered and adopted out.

Two bedrooms in Tara's home are now dedicated to foster cats—one is a kitten nursery and the other a kitty playroom.

Tara's pinup activities were overrun by cats and kittens. She has a pink pinup cat tattooed on the inside of her right arm, and her pinup photos now include cats and kittens.

Besides fostering, Tara cares for a colony of feral cats at her home in Dorr. She calls them *feeder friendly*— they're friendly to her only because she feeds them. Tara's an outspoken defender of feral cats. When feral cats were being trapped and killed at Sandy Pines, a nearby resort, Tara organized a crowd to attend a township meeting in defense of the cats.

Tara's husband, Jonathan Richard (Jon or Ricky), is supportive of her cat activities. He likes to drive and helps transport cats as needed. He's also been known to bring home cats from a known dumping area near their home. The couple has one daughter and three granddaughters.

Tara's love of rescuing pregnant cats and raising the babies continues. Her "B Litter" came from Sugar, a pregnant cat found at the home of a neighbor of Tara's uncle. There were three Sugar Babies: Bailey, Blossom and Bitty. After they were raised and adopted, Tara took on a bigger challenge—two cats, a mother-daughter duo.

"They were both heavily pregnant," she said.

The daughter, Melody, gave birth to five kittens. Six days later the mom, Harmony, birthed seven kittens.

"I had a 12-kitten orchestra," Tara said. They were Litters C and D.

Litter E came from Eden, who gave birth to seven black kittens nicknamed the Pudge Panthers. They were all named after characters from the Bible whose names started with E.

Next came Mama Fae and her eight Flockers, all of them brown tabbies with white markings.

Tara hit a snag with the G Litter. All four kittens were orange so she named them the Golden Globes and named them after movie stars. One was too small to survive.

The mother of the Globes came from a hoarding situation where all the cats were orange—generations of inbreeding was suspected. Two of the remaining kittens were fine and found homes. The fourth kitten, Gillian, was diagnosed with FIP.

Feline infectious peritonitis (FIP) is a viral disease in cats caused by certain strains of a virus called feline coronavirus. Thanks to Dr. Niels Pedersen and his team of researchers, the discovery of the use of antiviral drug GS-441524 has revolutionized FIP treatment. What was once a fatal disease is now treatable.

The treatment consists of a daily injection for 84 days. Dosage is determined by weight. Gillian weighed a pound when she was diagnosed. Her dosage increased as she gained weight. Tara estimated she would need 13 vials of the drug at a cost of $845. On her Touch of Cats Facebook page, Tara started a fundraiser to cover the expense of the medication and raised $1,000. Another fundraiser will cover veterinarian visits and bloodwork, which has to be done every four weeks.

Tara gave Gillian the injections herself and struggled with leakage and bleeding.

When the injections are completed, there is an 84-day observation period. If there isn't a relapse during that time, Gillian will be considered cured. Then she will be spayed, vaccinated and available for adoption.

"I hope there's a special somebody out there for her," Tara said, adding that she's emotional when she adopts out her kittens. "It's sad, but it's sadder if they die. Their lives are more important than my sadness."

As much as she would love to keep Gillian, Tara's going to try hard not to make her the couple's ninth cat. "I'll let the universe decide how it will play out," she said.

You can follow Tara's foster adventures on her Facebook page, Touch of Cats. To learn more about cats diagnosed with FIP, go to www.fipwarriors.com.

Tina Nicholes with Sweet Pea.

Rescue Addiction—a Natural High

Tina Nicholes of Muskegon has been involved in cat rescue for close to twenty years. "It's like the mafia. Once you're in, you can't get out," she said.

Tina's parents raised Manchester terriers, but she developed a passion for the "other" four-legged pet. That passion turned into an obsession after Tina's two children grew up and left home. As an empty-nester, Tina needed something to fill her time so she started volunteering for Judy Austin at Cat Tales Rescue in Norton Shores. She also lent a hand at Heaven Can Wait Animal Haven.

Tina cleaned, helped at adoption events, transported cats, fostered and whatever else she was asked to do. Volunteering resulted in Tina starting Weezy Cat Rescue with a friend, but when that co-founder got a full-time job, the rescue dissolved.

I met Tina when she was cleaning at Pay it Forward, a veterinary clinic for low-income pet owners. The clinic always seemed to be closed when I stopped to deliver magazines. If Tina was there, she would unlock the door so I could do the drop-off and we'd chat for a few minutes.

In 2013, Heaven Can Wait was called in on a hoarding case north of Muskegon. The police had been asked to do a welfare check on a man whose parents couldn't reach him. They discovered the guy dead in his home. They also found dozens of cats in the house and called the county animal shelter who then asked Heaven Can Wait for help. I was invited to observe for an article for *Cats and Dogs Magazine*—a cautionary tale about cats being prolific breeders and that help was available for pet owners to get their cats spayed/neutered.

Tina was one of the women helping catch the cats at the doublewide trailer that sat on a large lot in a secluded setting. Some cats were tame and easy to get into carriers. Others were scared and hid. The women discovered the cats could get beneath the trailer by squeezing through a hole near the kitchen sink plumbing. The space under the home was skirted but had an opening where they could get outside.

I watched as Tina rolled on a mechanic's creeper into the dim, confined crawl space under the house to set live traps. We'd go sit in the car for a while and then check to see if any cats had been lured into the traps by the smell of food.

The family of the deceased owner gave the rescuers a short deadline to remove the animals. In just a few days, close to 100 cats were caught or trapped, both in and outside the home. With no place to take so many cats, Tina temporarily housed 65 of them in her garage for three weeks until Heaven Can Wait found a place to rent.

With an obsession for cats, a big heart and access to Facebook, Tina began to answer pleas for help with strays.

"Momma got out of control," she said.

Tina had 125 cats in her home when she realized she had become a cat hoarder. The City of Muskegon was on the verge of condemning the house she and her husband, Hal, had lived in for close to 40 years. Hal was threatening divorce, and she was about to lose guardianship of her 12-year-old grandson, who had lived with the couple since birth.

Child Protective Services told Tina to get rid of her cats and even suggested euthanasia. About that time, Tina discovered she had cancer and underwent a full hysterectomy.

The stress of it all caused Tina to have panic attacks. "Cats were my therapy," she said. She turned to her friends in rescue, and they stepped up and took her adoptable cats.

"That left me with the unwanted misfits," she said. The cats who were shy, old or had medical problems making them unadoptable.

The primary problem with the house was the cats had peed on the carpeting, and it was beyond cleaning. The smell was unhealthy to breathe. The flooring needed to be replaced. When the project began, a layer of tile that contained asbestos was discovered. The asbestos was a biohazard, so Tina and Hal and the remaining cats had to move out of the house for three weeks. Tina was able to get a grant from the City of Muskegon to replace the hazardous flooring. The new floors prevented the house from being condemned, but it didn't stop Tina from losing her grandson.

"We didn't get it done in time and they took him anyways," she said. The young boy went to live with his dad, but Tina was able to visit him every other weekend.

Despite all the problems that rescuing cats caused in her life, Tina continues to rescue. "It's a natural high. I feel good when I help a cat go to a better home," she said.

Most of what she does now is networking on Facebook. She belongs to several Michigan-based rescue groups and when she spots a post regarding a cat requiring urgent help she shares it and tags her rescue friends.

"It takes a village," Tina explained. She has developed a network of like-minded friends who work together to save the lives of countless cats.

"To help cats is a feel-good pill," she said.

Sometimes Tina still takes in a cat or two. She has developed relationships with a handful of local organizations that have adoption programs, such as Noah Project, Muskegon Humane Society and Faithful to Felines. When her cats are ready for adoption, she'll place them on the groups' waiting lists. When they have an opening, they contact her.

Tina now exercises self-control. "I've learned to say no," she said, adding that she tries to keep the number of cats in her care under 20 but admits that number creeps up in the winter when there are so many cats found outside in life-or-death situations.

As for her husband, Tina said after 40-plus years of marriage, he's learned to live with her bringing cats into their home. "He doesn't mind them coming as long as they go," she said, which is good because Tina plans on being involved in cat rescue until she can no longer physically do it.

Debra Westerhof and three of the babies she bottle fed.

Bottle-Feeder and Feral Cat Crusader

"If they don't come to you, they'll die," the shelter staffer told Debra Westerhof. When orphan kittens are brought into an animal shelter, time is critical. At Harbor Humane Society in Ottawa County, the go-to person for vulnerable kittens is Debra. In this case, two, two-week-old kittens were malnourished and covered with fleas.

"How do you say no?" Debra asked.

She can't, and she didn't.

The babes were so sick they wouldn't even take a bottle and had to be force-fed. No problem. Debra's prepared for every scenario. The closet in her office is filled with everything required to take care of motherless kittens, including a heart-beat kitty—a stuffed cat with a battery-operated heart.

"Babies love it," she said. The little ones cuddle into the fake fur and are soothed by the rhythmic beat of the imitation heart.

Debra has been the surrogate mom to more than 450 orphaned kittens. In 2017, she quit keeping track of the number of kittens she has mothered, but she hasn't stopped saying yes to helping.

"It's my niche," she said. "I love feeding the babies." She claims it lowers her blood pressure, but that still doesn't make her fond of three a.m. feedings.

Kittens younger than two weeks of age have to be fed every two to three hours. When they hit the two-week milestone, the feedings are shifted to every three to four hours.

"I have no life when I'm bottle feeding," Debra said. Each kitten takes 10 to 15 minutes to eat. At about four weeks, they are offered kitten chow but are still given a bottle to ensure they're getting enough nourishment.

The kittens stay with Debra until they are adopted.

Debra's path to becoming a bottle-feeding expert started fourteen years ago when a stray cat had kittens under her deck. That cat, named Mama Boots, became sick and couldn't be saved. Her death left Debra with five orphans.

Debra is the owner of Pine Ridge Assisted Living Facility in West Olive, Michigan. Her home adjoins the facility, and taking care of the residents is more than a full-time job for her. A volunteer from the local humane society, who regularly brought shelter animals to visit the residents, advised Debra on how to care for the motherless kittens. All five survived. Debra kept three while a friend adopted the other two.

The incident changed her life—Debra became aware of the plight of motherless kittens and the desperate need for foster care so she started volunteering for the humane society. Her work allowed her the flexibility required for taking care of kittens. Plus, the residents of Pine Ridge helped socialize the youngsters—getting them accustomed to humans and used to being handled.

"The residents enjoy it. It's part of their day," Debra said.

Debra was a volunteer at Harbor Humane Society when I met her. Soon afterwards, I discovered she owned an assisted living facility where the residents helped her take care of kittens, which sounded like a great story. So, I went and interviewed Debra and a few of the residents. At the time I visited, they were without kittens. The last batch had been adopted, and they were praying for more to be delivered. An easy prayer for God to answer.

After five years of volunteering for Harbor Humane, Debra was invited to become a board member. Her love of cats was instrumental in Harbor Humane changing their philosophy on how they handled feral cats. In the past, feral cats were routinely euthanized when they were brought in. Now they are spayed or neutered, vaccinated and, when possible, returned to where they were caught.

TNR stabilizes a cat population, and over time, the number of animals will decrease. It also improves the cats' health by ending the stresses associated with mating and pregnancy. Debra explained that eradicating cats from an area doesn't work long-term. Studies show that removing feral cats from an area creates a vacuum effect: cats from neighboring areas move into the newly available space to take advantage of food and shelter. Of course, these cats breed and before long the number of cats in the area will once again be high.

Thanks to Debra, feral cats who can't be returned to where they are caught are now released behind the humane society facility where there are sheds and cathouses for shelter. Staff from Harbor Humane provide food and water.

Debra said sometimes cats thought to be feral turn out to be somewhat friendly but still aren't suitable as house cats. Those animals are available for adoption to people who have barns and need rodent control.

As a board member and volunteer for Harbor Humane, Debra became aware of the plight of outside cats. She realized there was a need beyond what the humane society could do.

Seven years ago, Debra, along with three other women (Carleen Everett-Bauer, Sara Bennett and Christina DeConinck), started A Feral Haven. Their goal was to help community cats in Ottawa County.

Community cats are un-owned cats who live outdoors. They may be feral or lost or abandoned pets.

A Feral Haven loans traps to people who are willing to live-trap cats. They provide vouchers for free spay/neuter surgery and vaccines for the cats who are caught. When they have the resources, they also provide cat food to the caretakers of the colonies of community cats.

A Feral Haven helps 100 to 120 cats each year.

The group receives a lot of phone calls from people wanting to surrender their cats. Debra wishes people would take pet adoption more seriously—cats can live 20 years or longer

"It's a lifelong commitment," she said.

She also wished more people would volunteer, not just for pet organizations but for groups that help humans too.

"People have to start helping. If everyone did something, every organization would have more than enough volunteers," Debra said.

For more information on A Feral Haven visit www.aferalhavenmi.org.

Update: Debra retired from Harbor Humane Society's board in January 2022. She sold her business to her son and retired in northern Michigan.

Chapter 3

Everyone Can do Something

Whatever talent or ambition you have, it can be put to work to benefit homeless cats. Cat rescues are always in need of volunteers, supplies, and cash for veterinarian expenses.

If you have organizational skills, put together a fundraiser—the need for money is continuous in the world of rescue. Organize a humongous yard sale or online auction of donated goods. Organize a soup supper or pancake breakfast. If you have a flair for working with your hands, crochet, knit or sew toys and beds for cats or build a cat tree to be raffled off.

If you want to hang out with cats, volunteer to help at a rescue. Odds are you'll be asked to help clean, but between scooping liter boxes, mopping floors and dishing out scoops of kibble, you'll have the chance to cuddle and kiss on cats.

Everyone can do something to help cats. The opportunities are endless.

In this chapter, you'll meet women who put their talents and passions to work to help cats in unique ways.

Sallie Alberts

Advice from an Intake Coordinator: Get Rid of the Boyfriend

Every night before Sallie Alberts goes to bed she says a prayer. "Dear God, please watch over all the cats who need homes, love and warmth, and bless all the people who are trying to save them."

Sallie wasn't always a fan of felines. When she was a kid, an incident with her aunt's black tomcat left her scratched and terrified. When she married, Sallie and her husband, Jim, adopted a cat named George, which helped her overcome her fear. After George died, a stray orange cat weaseled his way into their home. Orangey was a sweetheart who also weaseled his way into Sallie's heart.

"I started loving cats," Sallie said, adding she has always had a cat since those early days when George taught her not to be afraid. "Each cat is unique. I love their independence."

Sallie offered me a cup of tea after we had talked for a few minutes. Of course, I said yes. She told me to take a seat and then she sat the cutest teapot on the dining room table. The blue pot with its pink spout had faces of two whimsical, multi-colored cats painted on it.

"I love your teapot," I gushed.

Sallie then gave me a tour of her cat collectibles: a cat clock, cat mugs, a cat rug, a cat chalkboard, cat pillows and so much more. "If people give me a gift, it's something with a cat," she said.

"Me too," I told her. I felt right at home among her collection.

Sallie told me when they needed a cat sitter years ago they found Jeanine Buckner, owner of The Cat's Meow Pet Sitting and founder of Reuben's Room Cat Rescue in Grand Rapids.

Eventually, the couple adopted two Siamese littermates from Reuben's Room. "They walked in like they owned the place. We loved them," Sallie reminisced. Buster and Buddy were inseparable and loved people. They also loved boxes. Sallie has a photo album with photos of the brothers squeezed into every size box.

Sallie eventually started volunteering for Reuben's Room, doing laundry and brushing the furry residents. About 20 years ago, Sallie was promoted to Intake Coordinator. Her job was to talk to people who wanted to surrender their cats and make the difficult decision on which ones could be helped.

Reuben's Room was a no-kill rescue, which meant it was usually full with a waiting list of people wanting to re-home their cats. That made Sallie's job challenging.

Instead of saying, "Yes, we'll take your cat," which is what everyone wanted to hear, Sallie had to explain the rescue was full and the waiting list long. Most times she could only offer advice.

Sallie, in her late 70s and no longer driving, had the time to talk at length to each caller. She's handled up to a dozen calls in a single day, but the average daily call list was two to three.

She has heard all the excuses people have for wanting to get rid of their cat.

"My boyfriend moved in and he has a dog."

"My boyfriend doesn't like cats."

"My cat talks too much."

"My cat wants to sleep on the bed with me."

"My cat gets out when the grandkids come over."

"We're moving and can't take the cat."

"I found a box of kittens on the side of the road."

"The neighbors lost their house and left a cat outside."

"Grandma died and nobody wants her cat."

"The cat isn't using the litter box."

"I have 12 cats and can no longer afford them."

Sometimes Sallie doesn't say what she's really thinking—get rid of the dog or get rid of the boyfriend.

Sometimes her advice isn't what people want to hear—it's okay if the cat sleeps on the bed, spend more time with your cat and he won't meow as much, teach your grandkids to be responsible.

Sometimes people just need someone to talk to and are open to suggestions on how to solve their problem.

When it's a behavioral issue, Sallie tells them to think like a cat.

"You have to think where your cat is coming from," she explained. "Cats are smart. They have their own minds."

One person said their cat kept peeing in the basement. Sallie told them to move the litter box to the basement. Maybe the cat needed privacy and a quiet place to do its business.

Sallie laughed as she recalled the saying, "Dogs have masters. Cats have staff."

Once in a while people call back to tell her they followed her advice and that it worked.

"I feel good when I help someone," she said.

Sallie keeps a log of all the calls, and it has paid off. Once she was able to connect a woman who wanted to re-home a white deaf cat with a woman who had called months before wanting to adopt a deaf cat.

"It worked out nicely," she said.

In some situations, she doesn't have a solution to offer. In those cases, she tells people she'll pray for their cat.

Some conversations Sallie can't get out of her head.

One such call came from a building inspector in Sparta. A cat had gotten into the overhang of a new house and could be heard meowing. Was there anyone who could come get the cat out? Sallie told him no, they didn't have anyone to go out on calls. The builder was considering placing ammonia drenched rags in the overhang thinking it would force the cat out. Sallie thought the fumes would kill the cat. She never heard how the story ended.

Another call that haunts Sallie came from a man who had lost his home and was living in a motel. He had two, three-year-old littermates who had been with him since they were kittens. He was moving to a homeless shelter that didn't accept pets. A friend had agreed to take the cats but backed out at the last minute. When Sallie called him back he had already moved to the homeless shelter and had abandoned the cats in the woods near the motel.

"If I would have had a car, I would have been out there looking for those cats," she said.

Sallie called me after that incident and asked if I'd write an article for *Cats and Dogs Magazine*. She wanted people to know that it was better to take a cat to the humane society than to let it loose to fend for itself. That there were too many dangers for a house cat if it's dumped outside, be it in the city or country—cars, hunger, thirst, cold, dogs, wild animals, cat-hating people and more. I suggested she write the article, which she did. It was published in the Fall 2018 issue.

Sallie has accepted the fact that she can't help all the cats people call about. All she can do is her best.

Five years ago, a woman called who was moving to Washington and didn't want to put her cat through a long car ride. At the time, Sallie had just divorced her husband after 46 years of marriage, Buddy and Buster had both passed, and for the first time she was alone. She decided to adopt the woman's cat.

So, Will came into her life. She was told Will was born with a heart murmur and wasn't expected to live, but the little guy had a "will" to live.

Will had separation anxiety and would panic whenever Sallie got her shoes out of the closet. She recalled how he would cry endlessly when he thought she was leaving.

Sallie worked with the anxiety-ridden cat. She'd put on her shoes and tell him, "I'll be right back." She'd go for a short walk in the hallway of her apartment complex and then return. She did that until he quit crying when she got her shoes out. She continued to leave for brief outings until he learned she always returned. Now she usually has to wake Will to tell him when she's leaving. She laughed as she said he always gives her a silent meow as if saying goodbye.

When asked if she was a crazy cat lady, Sallie hesitated. After thinking for a few seconds, she agreed to the label.

"I honestly believe I am crazy," she said. She admits she has read poetry and the *Bible* to her cats. Years ago, she bought a video on how to massage a cat. She claimed her cats loved being massaged and it helped build trust.

When her cat Charley had asthma and cancer, she used to rock him in a rocking chair like a baby. She used to warm a towel in the dryer to cover him.

"The happier you make your cat, the happier they make you."

Sallie and Will both seem extremely happy.

Helen Hamler with Cross-Eyed Joe.

A Lifetime of Cats

Helen Hamler has had a thing for cats her entire life. Now retired and assisting her husband, Roger, recover from a traumatic brain injury and helping care for her elderly mother-in-law, Helen's limited on what she can do to help cats. What she does do is what every cat rescue desperately needs.

"We try to be supportive financially," Helen said.

One of the cat rescue groups Helen helps is Cannonsville Critters, which she learned about from reading *Cats and Dogs Magazine*. At the time, Helen was advocating for cats at the Montcalm County Animal Shelter.

"Every week I'd go there to pick out a cat to sponsor," she said. Sponsoring a cat made adoption more affordable.

It was at the shelter that Helen first met Michelle Hocking, the co-founder of Cannonsville Critters. Besides a love for cats, the women discovered Michelle's aunt was Helen's best friend in high school.

Helen now serves on the Board of Directors for the nonprofit and supports the group however she can. Back when she had time, Helen fostered cats and kittens. She was also a fixture at most fundraisers. She has a garage the group uses for storage, and she pays for the rescue to have a full-page ad in every issue of *Cats and Dogs Magazine*.

Helen was born and raised in Montcalm County. The rural county, made up of small towns and farmland, has always had an abundance of cats. When Helen was young, she fed strays, but having cats spayed or neutered wasn't even a consideration.

"Back then, vets worked on cows and pigs. Nobody took their cat to a vet," she recalled.

Helen lived with her parents on Clifford Lake for 50 years. A shed on the family's property was home to the neighborhood strays, and Helen and her dad provided the meals. When the Hamler family moved to Stanton, they sold the lake property on a land contract. Until the contract was paid off, they continued to care for the cats who lived in the shed. But one-by-one, the cats moved on. When there was only one left, it was caught and brought to the family's new home.

Helen worked for the Montcalm Intermediate School District for 45 years. She started as a secretary but worked her way up to Associate Superintendent of Finance. It was a job she loved, and she brought her passion for cats with her to work.

An orange and white cat frequently hung out by the entrance to the administration building. Someone let the cat inside and soon the kitty's visit became routine. Helen started feeding the guest—you know what they say, *if you feed a cat, it'll come back*. Since Helen fed him, he was often found in her office making himself at home lounging on papers, as cats love to do.

But the cat wasn't homeless. Came the day when someone stopped by and asked, "Do you have my cat?" Turned out the cat's name was Raffey and he belonged to a family who lived next door. The neighbor's kids would sometimes come and get Raffey, but he always returned.

"He was a character," Helen said.

If people left their car windows down in the parking lot, Raffey would jump in and make himself at home. One visitor almost had a heart attack as he was driving away from the building and Raffey jumped from the back seat to the front.

Then a school official saw Raffey and declared that having a cat in the building was not acceptable. Helen thought Raffey would be expelled, but when the school superintendent talked to her he only asked that Raffey be confined to her office. After that Raffey was escorted to Helen's office where he had plenty of food and love.

When Helen retired, her coworkers suggested she approach Raffey's owners and ask if she could have him. The owner told Helen she might as well take him since Raffey spent more time with her than he did at home.

"I was excited to think they would let me have him. It made the decision to retire easier," Helen said.

Helen lived with her parents until she married at the

age of 52. She had dated Roger when they were in high school, but after graduation he left for West Point and she stayed behind. As a widower with four children, Roger moved back home so his mother could help with his young kids. After dating for two years, Helen and Roger married. The couple now have five grandchildren with another on the way.

What to do with empty bedrooms as the kids left home was never a problem—Helen filled them with cats.

When Helen's parents died, she kept their house and moved cats into it. Everyday she'd go visit and care for the spoiled kitties. But tragedy struck in 2019. While Roger and Helen were out of state at a conference, an electrical fire started in the basement of the home. The fire department saved most of the house, but several cats died from smoke inhalation. Volunteers from Cannonsville Critters took three surviving cats to the Sheridan Animal Hospital, but they weren't equipped to care for three seriously injured cats. Two were transferred to an emergency pet hospital in Grand Rapids, where one later passed. Another survivor was found hiding behind a dryer where there was fresh air from the dryer vent.

"It was devastating," Helen said. "I lost my family—all were strays or unadoptable cats from the shelter."

Helen had the house restored. The 13 cats who died are memorialized with their photos and names in a framed picture hanging on the wall in the house. Included is the inscription, *Heartbroken—you were so special. Loved you and miss you. See you at the Rainbow Bridge.*

Helen was informed by city officials that homeowners are only allowed to have three cats. Today the three survivors, Perdita, Mew and Mr. Beauty, continue to live at the house.

Shortly after the fire, Cannonsville Critters took in twelve cats from Keeper Kitties in Wayland when founder Sharon Lee was no longer able to care for them. Helen provided them a temporary place to stay in one of her rental houses, but eventually took them to her home where they live in an enclosed porch. Two have been adopted and one has passed from cancer.

"They kind of took the place of the cats I lost," she said.

Kati Dodge in the cat lounge with some of the adoptable
cats at the Happy Cat Café.

Coffee and Cats

Taking an entrepreneurial class in college changed the course of Kati Dodge's life. Instead of following her biology major, she veered in a different direction.

"After taking the class, I knew I wanted to have a business," she said. Kati just didn't know what type of business she wanted. By chance, she stumbled upon an article about a cat café in Japan—it caused a lightbulb moment. Maybe a cat café was her calling.

Kati always loved cats. At get-togethers with extended family, she remembers everyone sharing cat stories. "It was a great way for the family to bond."

To see if there was an interest in a cat café in West Michigan, Kati started a Facebook page about the idea. In one week, the page had close to 3,000 likes. The response inspired Kati. In the summer of 2015, she launched a Kickstarter campaign.

On August 17, 2017, more than two years after its conception, the Happy Cat Café opened. "It was tough, but

I was absolutely happy. The first two weeks we were completely booked," Kati said.

Tough was a mild word to describe the journey from dream to reality. Just finding a location for the café was a challenge because of state, city and county regulations. To have cats, the café had to be a registered animal shelter with the Michigan Department of Agriculture. The café also had to be located in an area zoned for animals. To serve coffee and food, the café needed to be licensed by the Kent County Health Department.

"The food code says no animals and there's no difference between a restaurant and a coffee shop," Kati explained.

In February 2016, Kati found a building on South Division just south of Wealthy Street in Grand Rapids. An engineer was hired to design separate ventilation systems for the cat room and the area where food would be served. Two entrances—one for cats and one for people, was also required.

When the café first opened only self-serve coffee and prepackaged snacks could be sold because the ventilation systems weren't up to spec. It would take close to four years before Kati could save the money to have the proper ventilation systems in place. In early 2022, the cafe finally received its food-service license, which allowed Kati to ditch the self-serve coffee machine and prepackaged snacks. Now visitors can enjoy specialty drinks such as glittery gato and raspberry paw prints. Also available are classic coffee and teas.

"People who stop for coffee are surprised to see cats. They think Happy Cat is just the name of the café," Kati said.

The café has two rooms. One has a counter for ordering, a small gift shop and tables with chairs. The other is a lounge for the cats. A large window separates the two rooms. The cat lounge is decorated with feline décor, comfy beanbag chairs, cat trees, and small tables with chairs. A built-in bench has space underneath where cats can escape when they need alone time.

There are up to a dozen cats in the lounge, all available for adoption. People can grab a specialty latte from the cafe and visit with the felines for 15 minutes or an hour. A standard hour-long visit costs $13. A 15-minute visit is $5.

The café offers group activities in the cat lounge such as coloring, crocheting and painting. All are fee-based and come with the possibility of cat participation. Private parties are also available.

Kati has partnered with various rescues to provide adoptable cats. Currently, she is working with Michele's Rescue, a non-profit, no-kill rescue also based in Grand Rapids. All cats are up to date with vaccinations, spayed/neutered, microchipped, and ready for a new home.

Since opening five years ago, Happy Cat Café has helped find homes for more than 550 cats.

Kati said cat cafés were first popular in Asian countries where the focus was sipping a beverage while playing with cats. In the United States, the cafés have morphed into adoption sites.

"There's a lot of stigma around shelters. Here you're seeing cats in a relaxed atmosphere—more like a home," Kati said. She attributes the home-like setting to the high number of adoptions.

Kati's dream for the future is to open a second location and to expand the gift shop, which focuses on items for cats and cat lovers.

She describes the experience of starting and running the café as transformative.

"I've met some incredible people in rescue. I work on the rosy side of rescue—with healthy cats ready to adopt. I couldn't do what the rescues do, but I want to be supportive," she said.

For more information on the Happy Cat Café, 447 S Division, Grand Rapids, visit www.happycatgr.com or follow them on Facebook or call 616-202-4750.

Jackie Overkamp
with her *Can Queen* trophy.

The Queen of Cans

Twice a week you'll find Jackie Overkamp at a Meijer store feeding cans and bottles into a bottle-return machine. At the end of each five-hour stint, she'll have racked up $300 to $400 in cash receipts.

When Jackie retired four years ago, she started volunteering for Noah Project, a no-kill pet rescue in Muskegon. A big time cat lover, Jackie was happy to help with adoptions at Petco and clean cat cages at the store.

During the Covid-19 shutdown, adoptions stopped at the pet supply store leaving Jackie with spare time. She noticed bottle return operations at grocery stores also stopped. Jackie took advantage of the situation and put a sign outside her home offering to take neighbors' cans and bottles—she would store the empties and return them when things opened again. Her intention was to raise money for local animal rescue organizations.

"My husband just shook his head. I told him not to worry," Jackie said.

When stores started accepting bottles and cans, Jackie began returning the ten-cent treasures. She divided the proceeds, close to $300, between Noah Project, Faithful to Felines and Heaven Can Wait.

Noah Project also collected cans and bottles during the pandemic and stored them in garbage bags behind their shelter. Jackie volunteered for the monumental task of cashing in the stockpile of returnables. She put a tarp in the back of her Jeep and piled in the bags. At Meijer, she was only allowed to bring in one shopping cart of bags at a time.

Jackie did two Jeep loads each day. She timed herself and found she could empty a garbage bag in eight minutes.

Jackie said people in the bottle return area often comment on the number of cans and bottles in her cart. When she explains the money is going to help animals at Noah Project, they sometimes give their empties to her.

Jackie was surprised when she was presented a trophy for her work by Noah Project's Board of Directors. The trophy was a bottle on a stand with a plaque that read, "We will always be thankful for your efforts." The bottle had an emblem with a crown dubbing Jackie the *Can Queen*.

On her Facebook page, Jackie continues to ask people to donate their cans and bottles. She offers a pickup service and has established a regular clientele. She has since raised another $3,700 for Faithful to Felines.

Noah Project also continues to ask for returnables.

"They just keep coming," Jackie said. And she keeps loading her Jeep and driving to Meijer.

Jackie has returned more than $100,000 worth of cans and bottles.

Returning cans and bottles isn't the only thing Jackie does to help animals. She's a firm believer in spay/neuter and offers to transport people's cats to C-SNIP's Lakeshore facility in Fruitport.

In 2021, she transported 60 cats. As of mid-July 2022, she had already transported 72 cats. On Facebook, she posts the photos of the cats she takes in for surgery with a comment such as, *they won't be making any more babies.*

The cost to the cat owner for the spay/neuter surgery is $20. A grant pays the remaining $30. Jackie donates her time and gas.

When asked why she does so much, Jackie answered, "I love animals. I want to help the voiceless who can't help themselves."

Back Row: Lori Sarki (left), Carol Orr, Chris Gara, Michelle Elliot, Carolyn Benes

Front Row: Eileen Slagter (left), Jackie Barter, Eva Sims

Crafters

Hands for Paws began in 2010 with six volunteers from Harbor Humane Society in Ottawa County. The women shared a love for animals and crafting and began making beds and toys for use at the shelter. Soon they began selling crafts at local pet events.

Over the years they have donated thousands of dollars in cash and crafts to local humane societies and animal rescue groups. Members donate their time and materials so 100 percent of the proceeds go directly to animal welfare.

In 2022, Hands for Paws had eight members including the original six.

"Over the past 12 years, we have become good friends," said leader Jackie Barter. When Jackie moved from Holland to Grand Rapids, she remained active in the group. "These ladies are so gifted and creative that just being with them boosts my spirits and sparks my enthusiasm to continue the work we do."

The women have a wide variety of skills and interests including sewing, knitting, crocheting, quilting, jewelry making, paper crafts, wood crafts and baking.

They make beds, cat hammocks, carrier liners, birdcage covers, a wide variety of toys and kitten warmers for Harbor's foster program. They also make items for humans: scarves, hats, pillowcases, quilts, jewelry, tote bags, zippered pouches and golf club covers.

Most items are donated to fundraising events where they are sold, auctioned or used as raffle prizes. Some of the group's crafts are available through members' Etsy shops: RinkyDinkTreasures, CastoffTreasures and Kitti-Corner.

The women work independently at their homes, making items as their time and budget allow. There is no pressure or required quota. They get together six times per year, on the first Monday of the even-numbered months. During the get-togethers they plan for upcoming events, share ideas, swap supplies and admire one another's latest creations. Between meetings, they stay in touch by email. During Covid-19, they suspended meetings for 16 months.

I attended one of their meetings in 2013 to gather information to write an article for *Cats and Dogs Magazine*. I was amazed at their skills, dedication and camaraderie. Everyone should have such a close-knit group of friends.

Over time, the women of Hands for Paws have donated to numerous rescue groups and shelters including Harbor Humane Society, Muskegon Humane Society,

Pound Buddies, Best Pals, Heaven Can Wait, Crash's Landing, C-SNIP and K-9 Camo Companions.

One member, Carol Orr, crochets catnip toys for cats. The small balls are stuffed with scraps of fleece fabric and made with scraps of yarn—the ultimate in recycling. Local veterinarians sell them in their offices and Carol makes visits as needed to refresh the inventory and collect the proceeds.

Carol has been making the toys since 1997 and guessed she has made thousands. She stopped keeping track of how many balls she has crocheted and how much money she has donated, but at one point it was close to $11,000.

Hands for Paws members like to recycle and repurpose. Member Carolyn Benes transformed an old quilt into stuffed animals and created a tag for each animal with the history of the material and the phrase: Comfort from Castoffs, Consider Adopting an Older Pet.

Another project involved hundreds of magnetic picture frames that staff at Harbor Humane Society offered to the group. The women decided to fill the frames with photos and names of adoptable shelter pets and place them on a "sponsor board" at Harbor's thrift store. For $3, the pet in the frame could be sponsored. The framed photo was given to the sponsor as a thank-you gift.

When a local hotel chain donated a huge box of chair back covers to the humane society, the donation was passed onto the women. "We tried our darnedest to use those things up, but they were a challenge," Jackie said.

The nondescript beige fabric was a strange synthetic blend with a chamois-like finish, making it almost impossible to sew by hand. The women combined the covers with recycled shirts to make patchwork pet beds. They used some to make cat toys.

Jackie said one of the most unusual requests came from Debra Westerhof of A Feral Haven. Deb fostered orphan kittens and often had several litters to bottle feed. She needed a way to keep the hungry kittens calm and occupied while awaiting their turn to feed.

"She asked if we could create a kitten pacifier," Jackie said. The women brainstormed and started with an oversized kitten warmer (a rice-filled microwaveable pillow) and covered it with Sherpa fleece to represent momma cat. Two rows of buttonholes were added along mama's "chest" and nursing bottle nipples were inserted through each hole.

"Our little deception worked like a charm and the kittens happily suckled on the soft, warm substitute mom," Jackie said.

Hands for Paws' philosophy is that everyone can do something to help animals. "We can't all donate huge sums of money, but we can donate a few hours of our time to volunteer at a shelter or help with a fundraiser or mass mailing. Rescue organizations operate on very tight budgets with minimal staff. They rely on volunteers for everything from cleaning and maintenance to clerical work. If you have a desire to help, there is a job you can do. And the rewards are priceless."

About the Author

Janet Vormittag is an animal advocate, author and publisher. She is the author of *You Might be a Crazy Cat Lady if ...* (volumes 1 & 2) and *The Save Five Series*.

In 2006, Janet founded *Cats and Dogs, a Magazine Devoted to Companion Animals*. This free publication, distributed in West Michigan, is dedicated to finding homes for rescue pets, promoting spay/neuter and celebrating the people who work and volunteer in animal rescue.

Janet has a bachelor's degree in journalism from Grand Valley State University and was a correspondent for more than ten years for *The Grand Rapids Press*. She's a member of the Cat Writers Association. She currently lives in West Michigan with more cats than she cares to admit.

www.janetvormittag.com

Also by Janet Vormittag

You Might Be a Crazy Cat Lady If ...

You Might Be a Crazy Cat Lady If ... (volume 2)

The Save Five Series

Dog 281 (Book 1)

More Than a Number (Book 2)

The Save Five Club (Book 3)

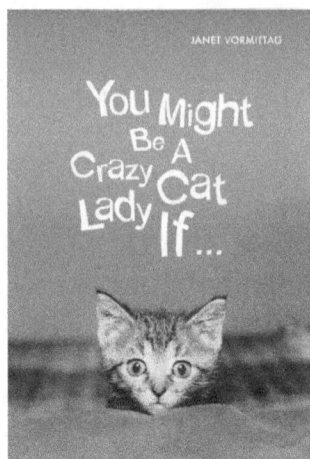

In this collection of humorous short stories, you'll meet the cats who kept the author sane during life's trying moments. Those same furry friends also drove her to the brink of crazy cat lady status. Janet questions if she's soft in the heart or soft in the head.

You'll meet more than 20 kitties, including Lucy who started Janet's love affair with cats. Lucy, a partially paralyzed kitty, competed with Janet for the house title of Best Mouse Hunter. Janet used a live-trap and practiced catch-and-release. Lucy's method was catch-and-eat, and she left only a trophy tail as proof of her prowess.

There are tales of Buddy, aka Basketball Cat, who couldn't say no to snacking; Wild Cat, who took more than a year to tame; and Frosty Flake, a foster kitten with attitude who never left. You'll also learn about Janet's trip to an animal shelter to pick up four kittens, which resulted in 16 kittens in carriers being packed into her car.

Each story features black and white photographs.

You Might be a Crazy Cat Lady If... takes the crazy out of the cliché Crazy Cat Lady and replaces it with compassion. It makes an ideal gift for anyone obsessed with our feline friends.

https://amzn.to/3qoXq9z

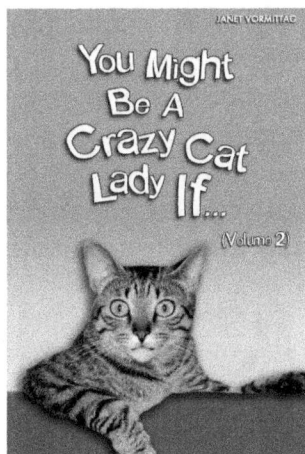

You Might be a Crazy Cat Lady If ... (Volume 2) is a collection of humorous and heartwarming short stories about the cats who share the author's home.

I promise I won't bring any more cats into the house.

That was the vow I made to myself when I realized I had too many furry four-legged friends. I won't reveal the exact number of freeloaders in my care, but I will admit I'm lousy at keeping commitments to myself.

I don't follow my own advice either. I'm good at telling other people what to do if a stray cat shows up on their doorstep: if you can't find its owner at least get it fixed. TNR, trap-neuter-return. But when a stray showed up on my porch, what did I do? I popped open a can of Friskies and named the visitor Fred. What do I have now? Kittens. Not sweet, adorable little fluff balls. Wild, mischievous hellions. Not only do I have unadoptable orphans, I have The Geriatric Club, soon to be The Assisted Living Club. After my divorce, when I found myself queen of my own home with no hubby limiting my cat intake, I went on an adoption spree. Those cuties are now senior citizens who require medications, demand canned cat food eight times a day and occasionally forget how to use a litter box.

The inn is full. The budget is bankrupt.

Maybe now I'll listen to myself.

https://amzn.to/3RUWyoU

The Save Five Series is a collection of fictional books that explore some of today's relevant animal issues, such as factory farming, medical and cosmetic research, dog fighting, animal hoarding and captive hunting preserves. If you have compassion for animals and love to read, you'll appreciate Janet Vormittag's heroic tales of Alison Cavera as she fights for animals who share this planet with us.

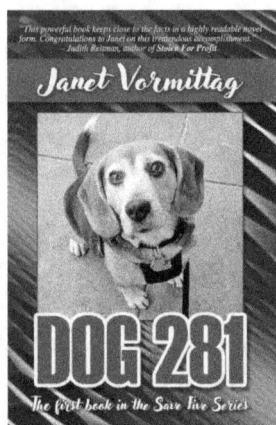

When her dogs are stolen, Alison Cavera will stop at nothing to find her beloved Cody and Blue. After breaking into Kappie's Kennel, Alison is relieved and nauseated by what she finds and is compelled to continue following the clues. To her horror, she discovers the unscrupulous world of dog theft and animal brokers.

This powerful novel reveals the practice of USDA Class B animal dealers selling pets to laboratories and universities for research.

Set in Michigan, *Dog 281* is the first book in the Save Five Series, which features Alison Cavera as she embraces a way of life that respects animals. Buried among the majestic maples, oaks and pines of the Manistee National Forest are secrets Alison Cavera needs to uncover.

https://amzn.to/3xdvmcQ

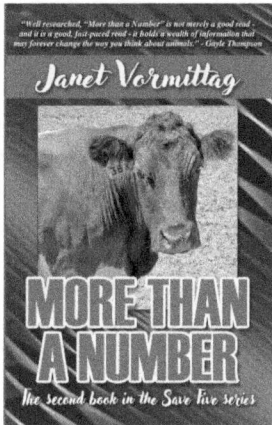

In the second book of the Save Five Series Alison has a new job at the county animal shelter. Helping homeless pets warms her heart, but the work isn't always as expected. Alison hadn't anticipated chasing a defiant dairy cow, being enamored with a farm sanctuary, discovering dozens of cats in a dead man's home or stumbling upon a barn with a blood-stained dog fighting ring. When the county sheriff refuses to investigate, Alison doesn't hesitate to follow the clues deep into the shadowy world of the illicit sport.

https://amzn.to/3QwRohK

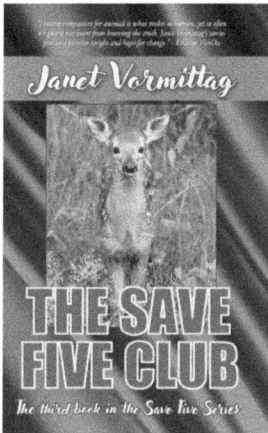

When Alison Cavera's moral compass doesn't align with the law, she dons a disguise and does what she believes is right. By light of the moon, this spunky animal activist cuts fences to free whitetail deer from captive hunting preserves. During one of her escapades, a camera silently records her illegal activity.

Alison struggles with what society finds acceptable and regrets she can't be the law-abiding woman her family and friends think she should be. Her inner battles take her down a dangerous path, one that could lead to prison or even death.

https://amzn.to/3L6f8b6

www.ingramcontent.com/pod-product-compliance
Lightning Source LLC
LaVergne TN
LVHW051401080426
835508LV00022B/2928